MODES OF ANALOGY IN ANCIENT AND MEDIEVAL VERSE

BY
PHILLIP DAMON

UNIVERSITY OF CALIFORNIA PRESS
BERKELEY · LOS ANGELES · LONDON

UNIVERSITY OF CALIFORNIA PUBLICATIONS IN CLASSICAL PHILOLOGY
Volume 15, No. 6, pp. 261-334
Issued August 18, 1961

UNIVERSITY OF CALIFORNIA PRESS
BERKELEY AND LOS ANGELES
CALIFORNIA

UNIVERSITY OF CALIFORNIA PRESS, LTD.
LONDON, ENGLAND

California Library Reprint Series Edition 1973
ISBN: 0-520-02366-8
Library of Congress Catalog Card Number: 72-95296
All Rights Reserved

PREFACE

IN HIS *Language as Gesture* R. P. Blackmur speaks of those junctures in literary history when given conventions, though still widely understood, no longer command a stable intellectual response and need to be "translated" into new imaginative terms. The following essays have as their theme the "translation" of three conventional tropes in ancient and medieval poetry: the long simile of Homer and his imitators, the personified landscape of Roman pastoral, and the nature parallelism of the medieval love lyric. I have tried to describe the uses of natural imagery in a few of the classic *loci* of each trope and to assess some of the conceptual and rhetorical demands to which these uses answered. I have then selected a later version of the trope and considered the ways in which the imagery and its analogical function changed as these demands lost some of their original force or were supplanted by new ones.

My texts are few and have been taken from periods widely separated in time because I have wanted to show a specific process within the conventions and not to characterize the conventions themselves. My aim has been to isolate and inspect some significant stylistic changes, and I have thought this better accomplished by attending critically to a few key texts ("test cases," as Erich Auerbach called the specimens in *Mimesis*) than by making a historical survey.

CONTENTS

I. Homer's Similes and the Uses of Irrelevance 261

II. Sappho's Similes and the Uses of Homer 272

III. The *Imago Vocis* in Vergilian Pastoral 281

IV. Echoes and Other Noises in the Later Pastoral 291

V. The Troubadour Nature Introduction and Some Other Descriptive Traditions 299

VI. Dante and the *Verace Intendimento* of the Nature Introduction 314

Appendix:
    Dante's *Canzoni* and the "Allegory of Poets" 329

Chapter I

HOMER'S SIMILES AND THE USES OF IRRELEVANCE

The tenuousness of the logical connection between the imagery and the point of likeness in many of Homer's long similes has usually been explained in familiar terms of artistic intention. Neoclassical criticism, both ancient and modern, has tended to consider the excursive images irrelevant and either to praise them as decorous embellishments or deplore them as excrescences.[1] Since the appearance of Hermann Fränkel's *Die homerischen Gleichnisse*, which stated without much qualification that these images were never irrelevant, it has been more customary to explore them for latent metaphorical connections and *Fernverbindung*, or at least to insist that they achieve an indirect relevance by adding "resonance" or "concrete vitality" to the comparison.[2] But disagreement about the Homeric simile's rhetorical basis has rarely disturbed the general agreement that its meaning structure is founded on a thoroughly Aristotelian approach to analogy as τὸ ὅμοιον θεωρεῖν. The currently fashionable search for "more remote and less obvious correlations," like the earlier search for the solitary, isolable *tertium comparationis*, starts from the premise that the only functional relation between a given image and the subject of the comparison is the relation of likeness.[3] Whatever the theoretical

---

[1] For a survey of neoclassical observations on the epic simile, see Samuel Eliot Bassett, *The Poetry of Homer* (Berkeley and Los Angeles: University of California Press, 1938), pp. 165–167.

[2] Hermann Fränkel, *Die homerischen Gleichnisse* (Göttingen: Vanderhoeck and Ruprecht, 1921). For examples of heavy emphasis on *Fernverbindung*, see Kurt Reizler, "Das homerische Gleichnis und der Anfang griechischer Philosophie," *Antike*, 12 (1936), 253. For "resonance," see Margarete Riemschneider, *Homer, Entwicklung und Stil* (Leipzig: Koehler and Amelang, 1950), p. 142. For "concrete vitality," see Bruno Snell, *The Discovery of the Mind*, trans. T. G. Rosenmeyer (Cambridge, Mass.: Harvard University Press, 1953), p. 199.

[3] The question of totemic identification as a conceptual nexus in the animal similes has sometimes been raised, but the answers have never been very enlightening. Wolfgang Schadewaldt, in *Von Homers Welt und Werk* (Stuttgart: Koehler, 1944), p. 147, n., writes: "Die ursprünglich magisch-sympathetische Identität von Verglichenem und Vergleich ist noch spürbar in Fällen wie *Il.* 16.259 ff., wo es nach einem Wespengleichnis heisst: 'deren (der Wespen) Herz und Mut habend ergossen sich die Myrmidonen aus den Schiffen.' Hinter dem Vergleich des heranscherrenden Pfeils mit einer Stechfliege (4.130) steht, dass der Pfeil noch eine Stechfliege 'ist.' " It is unhelpful to be told, without further specification, that a given idea lies "behind" a Homeric expression. Behind may be, to adapt a phrase of T. S. Eliot's, a great way back. As a look at William Empson's *Seven Types of Ambiguity* will show, the syntactical peculiarities that Schadewaldt finds in Homer's similes can also be found in Shakespeare's and Shelley's. Using Homer's peculiarities as evidence of totemic influence is simply begging the question. H. V. Routh, in *God, Man, and Epic Poetry* (Cambridge: University Press, 1927), seems on firmer ground in maintaining (vol. 1, p. 29) that totem simply is not an operative idea in Homer. But he favors *mana* as a key to the long simile's structure, and this leads him into the clearly mistaken notion that the extended similes are older than the short comparisons.

virtues of this premise, it cannot be said to have encouraged a very practical working approach to that large class of similes in which the basic comparison and its epiphoneme are both included in an emphatic and presumably meaningful pattern which seems to have little to do with resemblance. I mean that type of simile whose most immediately accessible effect lies in an explicit antithesis—a kind of *volta* which scarcely suggests that Homer has, for whatever reason, dropped or forgotten his starting point, or that he is trying to achieve some subtle harmony of thought or feeling beneath a surface impression of obvious disharmony. An example of this type is the simile at *Iliad* 12.278, in which the stones the Greeks and Trojans throw at each other are compared to falling snow.

> τῶν δ', ὥς τε νιφάδες χιόνος πίπτωσι θαμειαί
> ἤματι χειμερίῳ, ὅτε τ' ὤρετο μητίετα Ζεὺς
> νιφέμεν, ἀνθρώποισι πιφαυσκόμενος τὰ ἃ κῆλα·
> κοιμήσας δ' ἀνέμους χέει ἔμπεδον, ὄφρα καλύψῃ
> ὑψηλῶν ὀρέων κορυφὰς καὶ πρώονας ἄκρους
> καὶ πεδία λωτοῦντα καὶ ἀνδρῶν πίονα ἔργα·
> καί τ' ἐφ' ἁλὸς πολιῆς κέχυται λιμέσιν τε καὶ ἀκταῖς,
> κῦμα δέ μιν προσπλάζον ἐρύκεται· ἄλλα τε πάντα
> εἴλυται καθύπερθ', ὅτ' ἐπιβρίσῃ Διὸς ὄμβρος·
> ὣς τῶν ἀμφοτέρωσε λίθοι πωτῶντο θαμειαί.

[And as snowflakes fall thick on a winter day when Zeus the counsellor launches a snowstorm, showing those arrows of his to men; and he stills the winds and continues to shed down snowflakes until he has covered the peaks of the high mountains and the steep headlands and the grassy plains and the rich fields tilled by men; and it drifts on the harbors and the beaches of the grey sea, though the wave breaks against it and keeps it off, but all other things it enwraps from above when the storm of Zeus drives it on; so their stones fell thick from both sides]

The first three lines suggest suddenness (ὅτε τ' ὤρετο) and martial violence (τὰ ἃ κῆλα); a personal antagonist is pelting hapless personal victims. The phrase πίπτωσι θαμειαί evokes the rattle and heavy fall of the stones. The complement of πίπτειν is often something like "to the ground" or "in the dust"; it usually connotes a dull thud. And θαμέες ordinarily modifies solid objects pushing or clashing against each other. Homer is, like the Psalmist ("yea, he sent out his arrows and scattered them"), describing a driving storm. The diction and the harsh sound of the lines emphasize Zeus' hostility and the destructive potentialities of falling snow. But the impression of violence subsides abruptly as the fourth line, with its soft sound pattern, introduces the image of snow drifting over a broad landscape. The phrase χέει ἔμπεδον reverses the kinetic implications of πίπτωσι θαμειαί. The verb χέειν generally denotes a soft flow of water, air, or mist; ἔμπεδον implies fixity or inertia rather than action. The accumulation of images and the cadenced repetition of καί achieve something like the hushed ostinato of the final scene of Joyce's *The Dead:* "It was falling softly on every part of the central plain, on the treeless hills, softly falling on the Bog of Allen, and, farther westward, softly falling on the dark mutinous Shannon wave." The contrast between the static and the dynamic is elaborately emphasized, and the similarities and the differences between falling rocks and falling snow produce an unmistakable rhetorical tension.

The ordinary kinds of analysis have, rather unreasonably, ignored this dominant impression as something accidental or merely superficial. Bowra, for example, chose this simile as a good example of the way in which Homer, having established a point of resemblance, "simply follows his fancy and develops the picture without much care for his reason in using it."[4] George Soutar felt that a poet with a keener eye for resemblances would, when comparing stones to snow, give the snow more "bite." Most of the images were, he felt, simply "inappropriate."[5] Such categories as background, dramatic relief, free association, and William Empson's fifth type of ambiguity have also been invoked to account for Homer's practice—all implying that the epiphoneme is unrelated to the logic of the comparison or inadvertently related to it.[6] Fränkel, on the other hand, in a rather Proustian analysis, vindicated the logic of the notorious detail in the eighth line by translating κῦμα . . . ἐρύκεται as "wird angehalten" and taking the point to be that "der 'Sturm' der Troer ruht nun, ihre anbrandenden Wellen—das alte Bild—ersticken im Steinhagel, den ihr Angriff . . . ausgelöst hatte; aber trotz äusserer Ruhe geht unermüdlich, unerbittlich der zähe Kampf der Geschosse fort, wie ein unendlicher böser Schneefall bei stiller Luft."[7] It has also been urged that the quiet, static scene supports the comparison by emphasizing "the grimness and steady determination of both sides."[8] Still another interpretation holds that the accumulated images represent a thematically relevant catalogue of Zeus' whole armory of κῆλα—a reminder of his per-

---

[4] C. M. Bowra, *Tradition and Design in the Iliad* (Oxford: University Press, 1930), p. 126.
[5] George Soutar, *Nature in Greek Poetry* (Oxford: University Press, 1939), p. 140.
[6] On "background," see J. W. Mackail, *Lectures on Greek Poetry*, 2nd ed. (London: Longmans, Green, 1926), p. 108. On "dramatic relief," see Bassett, *Poetry of Homer*, p. 166. On "ambiguity," see W. B. Stanford, *Ambiguity in Greek Poetry* (Oxford: Blackwell, 1949), p. 93.
[7] Fränkel, *Gleichnisse*, p. 111.
[8] Cedric H. Whitman, *Homer and the Heroic Tradition* (Cambridge, Mass.: Harvard University Press, 1958), p. 149.

vasive influence on human affairs.[9] Although some of these analyses manage to get the epiphoneme into a satisfactorily rational relation to the *tertium comparationis*, they do so, one feels, by ignoring in part the rhetorical fact succinctly described by R. H. Lattimore: "The ultimate effect is not one of likeness, but contrast."[10] Ultimate (i.e., patent and finally irreducible) effects are the normal vehicles of meaning in traditional oral literature; and the impression that (to quote Professor Lattimore again) the simile "ends by contradicting the effect which it was introduced to achieve," probably deserves more attention than it has received. The impression has been explained away so often that an attempt to explain it may seem slightly perverse, but there is external evidence to support the uncomplicated hypothesis that Homer may at times have seen the obvious logical tension in a simile as meaningful simply *qua* tension and not always as a means to some less obvious end.

It is probable, on both linguistic and archaeological grounds, that Homer's short epic comparisons are part of the old Mycenaean tradition and that the long similes are later Ionic accretions.[11] Indeed, the many similes which have late linguistic forms in the epiphoneme but not in the basic comparison strongly suggest that the Ionian minstrels were accustomed to use traditional comparisons as nuclei for their own expanded versions.[12] In view of the manifest oriental influence, both early and late, on the pictorial content of the similes,[13] there is nothing implausible in the occasionally voiced suspicion that the addition of the epiphoneme may have been inspired by Ionian contact with Anatolian literature.[14]

[9] Riemschneider, *Homer*, p. 149.
[10] *The Iliad of Homer*, trans. Richmond Lattimore (Chicago: University of Chicago Press, 1951), p. xliii.
[11] For the bibliography of this subject, see Michael Coffey, "The Function of the Homeric Simile," *American Journal of Philology*, 78 (1957), 113. For a more recent discussion of the evidence, see T. B. L. Webster, "Early and Late in Homeric Diction," *Eranos*, 54 (1956), 35; and by the same author, *From Mycenae to Homer* (London: Methuen, 1958), p. 233 ff. See also G. P. Shipp, *Studies in the Language of Homer* (Cambridge: University Press, 1953), p. 79.
[12] Webster, "Early and Late," p. 40.
[13] Discussions of oriental influence on the Mycenaean comparison may be found in Charles Autran, *Homère et les origines sacerdotales de l'épopée grecque* (Paris: Denoël, 1938–1944), vol. 2, p. 345 ff.; Cyrus H. Gordon, "Homer and the Bible, The Origin and Character of East Mediterranean Literature," *Hebrew Union College Annual*, 26 (1955), 43; F. Dirlmeier, "Homerisches Epos und Orient," *Rheinisches Museum*, N. F., 98 (1955), 18; Webster, *Mycenae to Homer*, p. 223 ff. Webster concludes (p. 227) that "the long Homeric simile (as distinct from the short comparison) does not seem to have any ancestors." This conclusion is, as I try to show, unjustified.
[14] Some of the biblical evidence has been discussed in summary fashion by Franz Dornseiff, "Das altorientalische Priamel," *Antike und alter Orient* (Leipzig: Koehler and Amelang, 1956), p. 387 ff. From this evidence he concludes that "die kleinasiatischen Rhapsoden diese Gleichnisform aus altvorderasiatischer Dichtung übernommen haben." Another poetic tradition which had its own long simile was the Sanskrit epic, but the Sanskrit similes have a different intention and effect from those of the eastern Mediterranean. J. Gonda, in *Remarks on Similes in Sanskrit Literature* (Leyden:

This suspicion has, however, been supported by only the slenderest Biblical evidence and has never elicited a demonstration that the epiphonemic simile might have been a significant convention in Near Eastern poetry. Yet the materials for a modest approach to such a demonstration are not entirely lacking. The poetry of the eastern Mediterranean, both before and after Homer, contains a number of "Homeric" similes; and their distribution suggests that the epiphonemic style of comparison may have begun, as did the device of *parallelismus membrorum*, in a normal hieratic locution of early Egyptian ritual, and developed from this into a more consciously cultivated literary device in later poetry.[15]

In the formulary utterances of *The Book of the Dead* there are many rudimentary epiphonemes which seem to be due less to stylistic artifice than to a special understanding of the category of relation. The logically inapposite details in such comparisons as:

Thy navel is the Tuat [the underworld] which is open, and which sends forth light into the darkness, and the offerings of which are *ankham* flowers,[16]

Thy two hands are like a pool of water in the season of abundant inundation, a pool fringed about with the divine offerings of the water gods,[17]

were probably conditioned to a large extent by practical, pre-poetic notions about the meaning of similarity. In funerary texts describing metempsychotic transformation, there is a strong and natural tendency to pile up random theriomorphic images after the copula *m* (the "as" of identification) in order to insist with maximum rhetorical force that the deceased has really become an animal. For instance:

I fly and I alight as a hawk which has a back four cubits wide, and whose wings are like mother of emerald of the south.[18]

I am the dog-headed ape of gold three palms and two fingers high, which hath neither arms nor legs and dwelleth in Memphis.[19]

Brill, 1949), p. 96, characterizes several *yatha . . . eva* similes as Homeric. But the long Sanskrit simile depends on a concentrated and explicit analysis of the comparison's logical ramifications, as at *Mbh*, 12.317: "As a man of determination and courage, while climbing a flight of stairs with a vessel full of oil in his hands, does not spill a drop of the liquid if frightened and threatened by persons armed with weapons, even so the yogi, when his mind has been concentrated . . ." This kind of condensed allegory does not seem to me at all Homeric.

[15] For a discussion of the beginnings of parallelism in Old Kingdom mortuary texts, see Pierre Lacau, "Sur le parallélisme dans les textes des pyramides et ailleurs," in *The Pyramid Texts*, ed. Samuel A. B. Mercer (New York: Longmans, Green, 1952), vol. 4, p. 157.
[16] *The Book of the Dead*, chap. 172. Budge's translation.
[17] *Ibid*. Budge's translation.
[18] *Ibid.*, chap. 77. Budge's translation.
[19] *Ibid.*, chap. 42. Budge's translation.

This kind of elaboration, which had a proper function in assertions of identity, appears to have exerted a conceptual pressure on assertions of similarity, and to have encouraged an extralogical accumulation of sensuous detail even when, as after the copula 'is, there was no question of consubstantiality. The motives behind this pressure are perhaps to be sought in what Cassirer called "the fundamental mythic law of the concrescence or coincidence of the members of a relation"—the primitive tendency to see qualities as external dimensions of essence and thus to feel that, in sufficiently formalized contexts, similarity implies identity.[20] As Henri Frankfort observed, the whole conception of analogy in the Pyramid Texts is informed by an attitude toward logical relations which "reduces the significance of distinctions while increasing that of every resemblance."[21] The logical category of likeness shades into the "magical" category of sameness, just as it does in the presentational analogies ("tropes in the form of action," Ortega y Gasset called them) of mythic ritual performances.[22] The distinction which these texts make between "is" and "is like" seems as tenuous and intermittent as that made, for example, in the mimetic rehearsals through which the Egyptian king, by imitating a god, became a god. In the following ascension utterance the image characteristically fluctuates between that of a man flapping his arms like a bird and that of a bird flapping its wings.

> N. ascends to heaven, to thee, O Re! The face of N. is as the face of falcons, the wings of N. are as those of geese ... N. moves his arms like a *smn* goose. N. flaps his wings like a kite.[23]

This partial fusion of categories takes many forms. One form appears in a common formula which describes the king as the son of the vulture Nekhbet of El-Kab.

> Your mother is the great wild cow who lives in El-Kab, the white crown, the royal headdress, she with the long feathers, she with the two hanging breasts.[24]

Three distinguishable images are involved: the feathers associated with the vulture, the cow as a mother symbol, and the goddess who nurses the king in the form of a woman. But the images are not kept distinct by the

---

[20] Ernst Cassirer, *Philosophy of Symbolic Forms*, trans. Ralph Mannheim (New Haven: Yale University Press, 1953), vol. 2, p. 64. This "law" is also formulated as "the law of the leveling and extinction of specific differences" in *Language and Myth*, trans. Susanne K. Langer (New York: Dover, 1946), p. 91.

[21] Henri Frankfort, *Kingship and the Gods* (Chicago: University of Chicago Press, 1948), p. vii.

[22] José Ortega y Gasset, *The Dehumanization of Art*, trans. Helene Weyl (Princeton: University Press, 1948), p. 27.

[23] Mercer, *Pyramid Texts*, vol. 1, p. 102.

[24] *Ibid.*, pp. 244, 297.

grammar of simile or the tension of metaphor. They collapse into a synthesis of specific differences: your mother is a cow is a bird is a woman. The observed likeness between the three has produced what Cassirer says likeness often does produce in mythic thought: "an area of logical indifference in which sensuous particulars continually merge with one another."[25] This feeling for the alogical implications of likeness may have encouraged the epiphonemic treatment of liturgical similitudes. In literature as in life, the processes of identification tended to absorb the processes of comparison and to impose a structure which does not fulfill the stricter demands of Aristotle's χωριστόν.

Whatever the conceptual basis of the practice may have been, there are plenty of later similes which look as if they had developed from the forms of Old Kingdom literature in much the same way that the stylistically sophisticated parallelism of

Let them melt away as waters which run continually ...
As a snail which melteth away, let every one of them pass away; like the untimely birth of a woman, that they may not see the sun[26]

developed from the spare (and, as Pierre Lacau has shown, grammatically functional) repetitive structure of Egyptian ritual texts like

N. has flown as a cloud to heaven like a heron;
N. has kissed the sky like a falcon;
N. has reached the sky like a grasshopper, which makes the sun invisible.[27]

A few specimens follow, the first two from a text written sometime before 1600 B.C.

O that thou mayst come to the sister quickly,
Like a horse belonging to the king,
Picked from a thousand steeds of every kind,
Chief of the stables;
It is distinguished above the others in its provender,
And its lord knows its paces;
If it hears the sound of the whip,
It knows no resting,
Nor is there any chief of the charioteers
Who can draw level with it ...

---

[25] Cassirer, *Symbolic Forms*, vol. 2, p. 69.
[26] Psalm 58.
[27] Mercer, *Pyramid Texts*, vol. 1, p. 163. Lacau ("Sur le parallélisme") has shown that passages like this are extensions of the literary language's normal sentence structure, and that this structure "correspond à une tendance générale de l'esprit égyptienne." The passage would mean, on this view, that the deceased has successively assumed three forms appropriate to his ascension, and has flown to, touched, and settled upon the heavens.

> O that thou mayst come to the sister quickly,
> Like a gazelle bounding over the desert;
> Its feet reel and its limbs are faint,
> And a panic has entered into its limbs;
> For a huntsman is after it,
> And hounds are with him,
> But they see not its dust,
> For it has taken a resting place like a [...];
> It has taken the river as a road.[28]

Another Egyptian text roughly contemporaneous with these, perhaps slightly older, reads:

Their sacrificial stones stand empty,
Like those of the dead who have perished on the quay,
Without leaving a survivor,
And afterwards the wave has taken hold of one end of them,
And the sun has done the same with the other,
And the fish at the water's edge hold conversation with them.[29]

The Canticles contain several familiar examples, two of them from the third chapter.

Thy teeth are like a flock of sheep which are even shorn, which come up from the washing, whereof every one bears twins, and none is barren among them.

Thy neck is like the tower of David, builded for an armoury, whereon there hang a thousand bucklers, all shields of mighty men.

Franz Dornseiff has pointed out the basically Homeric structure of what is, in effect, a series of exemplary analogies offered by the Voice from the Whirlwind in Job.[30]

Doth the eagle mount up at thy command and make her nest on high?
She dwelleth and abideth on the rock, upon the crag of the rock, and the strong place.
From thence she seeketh the prey, and her eyes behold afar off.
Her young ones also suck up blood: and where the slain are, there is she.

An Akkadian vision poem from a tablet inscribed around 600 B.C. describes the visionary's awakening in the following simile:

And like a man who has shed blood, who wanders alone in the marshes, and whom a bailiff has seized so that his heart pounds,

---

[28] Text and translation in Alan Gardiner, *The Chester Beatty Papyrus* (Oxford: University Press, 1935), vol. 1, p. 35.

[29] Text and translation in Adolf Ermann, "Gespräch eines Lebensmüden mit seiner Seele," *Abhandlung der Berliner Akademie, phil.-hist. Kl.* (1896), p. 43. Ermann interprets the obscure fourth and fifth lines in this way: "Die Leiche liegt am Ufer, halb im Wasser und halb im Trockenen; Fluth und Hitze haben sich um sie geteilt und sich jede 'ihr Ende' davon genommen."

[30] Dornseiff, "Das altorientalische Priamel," p. 387.

Or like a young boar just matured who has mounted on his mate while his intestines
   tumesce constantly and he ejects dirt again and again from his mouth and rear,
He seethed inwardly and uttered a loud cry.[31]

The evidence from Arabic literature is, of course, very late, but the earliest extant lyrics are the product of an oral tradition of considerable and perhaps great antiquity.[32] Both the *Mu'allaqat* and the *Hamasa* are full of similes like the following from the *Mu'allaqa of 'Antara* in which the poet compares his horse's stride to an ostrich's.

At eventide it is as though I am breaking the hillocks
upon an ostrich close-footed, that lacks for ears,
to which the young ostriches flutter, as herds of Yemeni camels
flock to the call of a barbarous, incomprehensible voice;
they follow after the crest of his head; he is like a litter
laid upon a sort of bier, and tented for them,
small headed, visiting his eggs in 'Dhul Ushaira.[33]

The *Mu'allaqa of Labid* develops the description of a running camel into a remarkable thirty-four line simile beginning,

                    Or shall I liken her to a wild cow, whose calf
the beasts of prey have devoured, lagging though true herd leader?
Flat nosed, she has lost her young, and therefore unceasingly
circles about the stony waste, lowing all the while
as she seeks a half-weaned calf, whose carcase the grey robber-wolves
in greed unappeasable have dragged hither and thither.[34]

If, as this sampling of the textual evidence may suggest, the Homeric simile had Anatolian antecedents, it is less likely to have entered the Greek epic as an Ionian invention ("von Homer selbst entwickelt")[35] than as an early orientalism—one of the traits borrowed from Eastern sources in response to what H. L. Lorimer calls "the new curiosity in Homer's audience aroused by vague rumours and strange tales of lands

---

[31] Wolfram von Soden, "Die Unterweltsvision eines assyrischen Kronprinzen," *Zeitschrift für Assyriologie*, N. F., 9 (1937), 1. The earthy image at the conclusion of the simile, *nis-ti-sú e-lu-ú ßb-bu-sú it-tan-am-pa-hu titta a-na pi-sú ù arkati-sú it-te-ni-is-si*, has been variously rendered by different translators. Von Soden and also E. A. Speiser in *Ancient Near Eastern Texts Relating to the Old Testament*, ed. J. B. Pritchard (Princeton: University Press, 1955), p. 109, make the suddenly awakened dreamer the subject of *it-tan-am-pa-hu*, and put the image outside the simile. Alexander Heidel, *The Gilgamesh Epic and Old Testament Parallels*, 2nd ed. (Chicago: University of Chicago Press, 1949), p. 135, more reasonably makes the boar the subject and translates as I have.
[32] On the antiquity of the tradition, see R. A. Nicholson, *A Literary History of the Arabs*, 2nd ed. (Cambridge: University Press, 1930), p. xxii, 75; and A. J. Arberry, *The Seven Odes* (London: Allen and Unwin, 1950), pp. 251–254.
[33] Arberry, *The Seven Odes*, p. 180.
[34] *Ibid.*, p. 144.
[35] Schadewaldt, *Von Homers Welt*, p. 150, n.

whose names had not wholly perished out of mind."[36] The new experience of the Ionian migrants appears to have had a roughly analogous impact on both the poetry and the plastic art of the eighth century. Allusions to Eastern artifacts and customs (Miss Lorimer lists these under the summary headings of arms and armor, dress, and domestic architecture) were incorporated into the basically "Achaean" cultural setting of the *Iliad* in much the fashion that the first oriental motifs were incorporated into the geometric decoration of Greek pottery.[37] Guided by traditional memories of extensive Bronze Age contact with the East, Homer expanded the old allusions and introduced contemporary ones in order to exploit his hearers' fascination with a new-found world which was both an exotic novelty and the background of the archaic cultural symbiosis so enigmatically portrayed in their own poetic traditions.[38] The similes have often been singled out as one of the focuses of this orientalizing tendency in the epic. Their imagery is sometimes quite strikingly drawn from the Eastern world, and some of the animal similes are clearly based on Eastern literary tradition.[39] It is reasonable to infer that the epiphonemic structure of the similes was part of this broad pattern of influence and that, like the other oriental details, it was a late product of the accretive processes by which Mycenaean heroic poetry "was reborn and to some extent reattired according to the fashion prevalent in each new generation."[40] The pure excursiveness of the similes may have been intended to work with their novel pictorial content in alluding to a region and a culture which were, both in terms of history and topical interest, profoundly important to the Greek epic tradition.

The irrelevance of the Homeric epiphoneme may, then, have functioned within the narrative in the same way that the frequent irrelevance of the traditional epithet and formula does. More than a blind acquiescence to convention was involved in Homer's often otiose, sometimes

---

[36] H. L. Lorimer, *Homer and the Monuments* (London: Macmillan, 1950), p. 100.

[37] For a discussion of analogies between style in the similes and style in Greek vase painting, see Roland Hampe, *Die Gleichnisse Homers und die Bildkunst seiner Zeit* (Tübingen: Niemeyer, 1952).

[38] Autran, *Homère et les origines*, vol. 3, p. 89, writes concerning this aspect of the epic: "C'est une dernière tentative pour relier, par leurs mille et un souvenirs traditionels, ces trois continents que la mer avait unis; qu'elle allait maintenant séparer. Le voyage d'Argo en Colchide, comme celui de Ménélas à Sidon et à Pharos: cette guerre de Troie même, où les héros de la terre de Dardanos s'affrontent en une ultime bataille avec leurs émules, souvent leurs propres hôtes, ou leurs parents lointains, venus d'Eubée, de Béotie, d'Attique, de Thessalie, du Péloponèse, de Locride, de Phocide, de Crète, de Salamine, d'Ithaque, de Rhodes, de Symé; cette guerre n'est-elle point, au même titre que ces itineraires intercontinentaux de marins, le symbole dramatique, douloreux, authentique cependant, d'une unité? Unité sous-jacente, invisible, mais tenace et profonde . . .?"

[39] See Webster, *From Mycenae to Homer*, p. 218.

[40] Denys L. Page, *History and the Homeric Iliad* (Berkeley and Los Angeles: University of California Press, 1959), p. 178. See also T. B. L. Webster, "On the Track of Mycenaean Poetry," *Classica et Mediaevalia*, 17 (1956), 149.

contradictory use of these petrified words and phrases. Their local application was often of less importance to him than their sheer aura of antiquity, their ability to relate their subjects, in C. H. Whitman's words, "to the large tradition of the epic past and give them thereby an added dimension."[41] Hence the error of attempting on principle to rationalize such paradoxes as the "starry" noonday sky or Ajax's "bronze" oxhide shield.[42] Homer's archaizing style is quite capable of accommodating and even valuing this kind of "inappropriateness."

The same criteria may apply to the imagery of his similes. He may be trying occasionally, by a striking juxtaposition of ὁμοῖα and ἐναντία, to emphasize the salient difference between an expansive oriental simile and its sparely functional Mycenaean counterpart. I do not mean that his long similes never achieve any (or indeed all) of the varieties of relevance that have been attributed to them, but merely that relevance does not need to be imposed upon them in a doctrinaire way. Homer may have seen irrelevance as meaningful. When, for example, one feels that the comparison of Hermes to a seagull takes an unexpected and slightly incongruous turn:

σεύατ' ἔπειτ' ἐπὶ κῦμα λάρῳ ὄρνιθι ἐοικώς,
ὅς τε κατὰ δεινοὺς κόλπους ἁλὸς ἀτρυγέτοιο
ἰχθῦς ἀγρώσσων πυκινὰ πτερὰ δεύεται ἅλμῃ,

[Then he sped over the waves like a seagull which among the fearsome swells of the restless deep hunts for fish and wets its heavy plumage in the salt water][43]

there is no a priori necessity to sublimate one's feeling by invoking such dubious critical concepts as dramatic relief or by violently extracting relevance from the image in the way Reizler does: "Dank ihr ist nun das Schnelle auch leicht, mühelos spielende Beherrschung. Hermes würde Fische fangen, wenn es ihm beliebte. Des Hermes Flug über das Meer praeludiert des Odysseus letzter und schwerster Fahrt, die fischfangende Möwe dem ungefügen hilflosen Floss."[44] Homer may conceivably be doing what he seems to be doing—wrenching the comparison away from an image suggestive of effortless flight to an image of a bird battling the waves for its dinner. In expecting his audience to respond to the leisurely inconsequence of the picture, he may well have felt that he was not simply experimenting with the epic style, but rather reinforcing it, as Greek minstrels had always done, with features drawn from a newly enlarged view of the epic tradition.

---

[41] Whitman, *Homer and the Heroic Tradition*, p. 114.
[42] For a discussion of these epithets, see Sir Maurice Bowra, *Homer and His Forerunners* (Edinburgh: Nelson, 1955), p. 112.
[43] *Odyssey*, 5.51.
[44] Reizler, "Das homerische Gleichnis," p. 258.

Chapter II

SAPPHO'S SIMILES AND THE USES OF HOMER

An answer to some of the problems surrounding Sappho's "anormal" use of nonvernacular epicisms has been provided by several recent demonstrations that she generally (and unsurprisingly) uses Homeric forms and formulas when she wants to evoke Homer—when rising, for instance, to the height of a heroic argument or reinforcing the tonal possibilities of an epic trope.[1] The heavy concentration of anormal forms in,

οἶον τὸ γλυκύμαλον ἐρεύθεται ἄκρῳ ἐπ' ὕσδῳ
ἄκρον ἐπ' ἀκροτάτῳ, λελάθοντο δὲ μαλοδρόπηες,
οὐ μὰν ἐκλελάθοντ', ἀλλ' οὐκ ἐδύναντ' ἐπίκεσθαι

[... as the apple reddens at the very end of a branch, and the apple pickers have forgotten it, or rather they have not forgotten it—they could not reach it]

seemed to Lobel to have no discoverable "rationale."[2] But G. P. Shipp seems at least on the track of a rationale when he observes that the lines "are, of course, a 'Homeric' simile."[3] A. E. Harvey concludes from a study of the epithets in Sappho's narrative fragment on the marriage of Hector and Andromache that "the linguistic licenses occurring in almost every line leave no doubt of a deliberately created Homeric tone."[4] This welcome evidence of Sapphic deliberation in the use of Homeric detail may have some bearing on the interpretation of the variously understood fragment numbered 96 in Lobel and Page's *Poetarum Lesbiorum Fragmenta*.

σαρδ ...
..... πόλλακι τυῖδε νῶν ἔχοισα

ὠσπ .... ὠομεν ....
σε †θεασικελαν αρι-
γνωτασε† δὲ μάλιστ' ἔχαιρε μόλπᾳ,

νῦν δὲ Λύδαισιν ἐμπρέπεται γυναί-
κεσσιν ὥς ποτ' ἀελίω
δύντος ἀ βροδοδάκτυλος σελάννα

---

[1] G. P. Shipp, *Studies in the Language of Homer* (Cambridge: University Press, 1953), p. 86 f.; A. E. Harvey, "Homeric Epithets in Greek Lyric Poetry," *The Classical Quarterly*, n.s., 7 (1957), 206; A. W. Gomme, "Interpretations of Some Poems of Alkaios and Sappho," *The Journal of Hellenic Studies*, 77 (1957), p. 255.
[2] Edgar Lobel, Σαπφοῦς Μέλη (Oxford: University Press, 1925), p. xxv.
[3] Shipp, *Studies*, p. 87.
[4] Harvey, "Homeric Epithets," p. 209.

πάντα περρέχοισ' ἄστρα· φάος δ' ἐπίσχει θάλασσαν επ' ἀλμύραν
ἴσως καὶ πολυανθέμοις ἀρούραις·

ἀ δ' ἐέρσα κάλα κέχυται τεθά-
λαισι δὲ βρόδα κἄπαλ' ἄν-
θρυσκα καὶ μελίλωτος ἀνθεμώδης·

πόλλα δὲ ζαφοίταισ' ἀγάνας επι-
μνάσθεισ' Ἀτθιδος ἰμέρῳ
λέπταν ποι φρένα κῆρ . . . βόρηται·

κῆθι δ' ἔλθην ἀμμ . . . ισα τόδ' οὐ
νῶντ' ἀ . . . υστονυμ . . . πόλυς
γαρύει . . . αλον . . . . . . τὸ μέσσον.

[... in Sardis ... often sends her thoughts here ... how we ... you a goddess incarnate (?) and your singing pleased her most. And now she surpasses the Lydian women as the rosy-fingered moon at sunset surpasses the stars around her, and she sends her light over the salt sea, and over the flowering meadows too, and the pleasant dew falls while the roses bloom, and the delicate thyme and the sweet smelling clover; and as she wanders so much, thinking of her love for gentle Atthis, her heart is heavy in her tender breast. Us to come there ... is noisy ... the space between]⁵

The diction of the central comparison has an unmistakably Homeric flavor. The dialect form of two common epic epithets, ἁλμυρός and ῥοδοδάκτυλος, is used; and πολυανθέμοις and ἀνθεμώδης are both cited by Leumann as examples of "nachhomerischen Ableitungen von einem homerisch-poetischen Grundwort,"⁶ as reminiscent of Homer as the authentic πολυανθής and ἀνθεμόεις would be. The phrase βρόδα κἄπαλ' ἄνθρυσκα καὶ μελίλωτος ἀνθεμώδης strongly recalls Homer's characteristic botanical triads: κλήθρη τ' αἴγειρός τε καὶ εὐώδης κυπάρισσος (*Odyssey* 5.64) or ὡς ὅτε τις δρῦς ἤριπεν ἢ ἀχερωΐς ἠὲ πίτυς βλωθρή (*Iliad* 13.389). The prefix ἀρι- which immediately precedes the simile is presumably Homeric; and the ring form of the simile, with βρόδα in the last phrase echoing βροδοδάκτυλος in the first, is also adapted from epic practice.⁷ The opening image suggests the beginning of the simile at *Iliad* 8.555:

---

⁵ Edgar Lobel and Denys Page, *Poetarum Lesbiorum Fragmenta* (Oxford: University Press, 1955), p. 78; text with commentary in Denys Page, *Sappho and Alcaeus, An Introduction to the Study of Ancient Lesbian Poetry* (Oxford: University Press, 1955), p. 87. My text does not follow either of these in all respects, but the only detail which affects my argument is my acceptance of the eighth line with Schubart's emendation of μῆνα to σέλαννα. This emendation has not been admitted to the text of *Poet. Lesb. Frag.*, and Page has obelized the whole line.

⁶ Manu Leumann, *Homerische Wörter* (Basle: Reinhardt, 1950), p. 20. See also A. Meillet, *Aperçu d'une histoire de la langue grecque* (Paris: Hachette, 1930), p. 174.

⁷ On ring form in Sappho and elsewhere in Greek lyric verse, see John G. Griffith, "Early Greek Lyric Poetry," in *Fifty Years of Classical Scholarship*, ed. Maurice Platnauer (Oxford: Blackwell, 1954), pp. 42; 66, n. 23; 69, n. 73.

> ὡς δ' ὅτ' ἐν οὐρανῷ ἄστρα φαεινὴν ἀμφὶ σελήνην
> φαίνετ' ἀριπρεπέα,
>
> [As in the heavens the stars show clearly about the bright moon]

and the image is developed in a typical Homeric period: two long, flowing cola followed by three short, rather nervous commata, as at *Iliad* 4.275:

> ὡς δ' ὅτ ἀπὸ σκοπιῆς εἶδεν νέφος αἰπόλος ἀνὴρ
> ἐρχόμενον κατὰ πόντον ὑπὸ Ζεφύροιο ἰωῆς·
> τῷ δέ τ' ἄνευθεν ἐόντι μελάντερον ἠΰτε πίσσα
> φαίνετ' ἰὸν κατὰ πόντον, ἄγει δέ τε λαίλαπα πολλήν·
> ῥίγησέν τε ἰδών, ὑπό τε σπέος ἤλασε μῆλα.
>
> [As from a watching-place a shepherd sees a cloud coming over the sea driven by the west wind, and as he watches it from a distance, it seems blacker than pitch to him as it moves over the sea, and it brings a storm, and he shivers to see it, and drives his flock to a cave]

Homer often uses this movement to underline rising action in his more dramatically conceived similes. Sappho uses it here to reinforce the transition from the slow play of the moonlight to the inanimate energy of the blossoming meadow, illustrating, perhaps, what Demetrius meant when he said that she could adapt even the most forceful poetic effects to the uses of lyric delicacy.[8]

Diction and development are both like Homer's, but the simile's most obviously Homeric feature is the apparent irrelevance of the moonlit sea, the dew, and the flowers. This epic expansiveness has often been found curious, and various efforts have been made to assimilate these images somehow into the lyric's subjective situation. Wilamowitz thought that they were included by way of background: we are to imagine Sappho and Atthis watching the moon cross the sea and meadows as they think of the absent girl.[9] Hermann Fränkel sets the scene on the mainland and describes the imagery as "ein Bild der Nacht, in der Arignota drüben ihrer Freundinnen hier gedenkt."[10] Snell (who also adopts Wilamowitz' untenable notion that the girl's name was Arignota) speaks of the "nostalgic picture of Arignota in Sardis during a summer night under a full moon."[11] Against these views it may reasonably be urged that this is not what the poem says. The moon and its

---

[8] Demetrius, *De elocutione*, 140.
[9] U. von Wilamowitz-Möllendorf, *Sappho und Simonides* (Berlin: Weidmann, 1913), p. 54.
[10] Hermann Fränkel, *Dichtung und Philosophie des Frühen Griechentums* (New York: American Philological Association, 1951), p. 248.
[11] Bruno Snell, *The Discovery of the Mind*, trans. T. G. Rosenmeyer (Cambridge, Mass.: Harvard University Press, 1953), p. 66.

associated images are part of a formal comparison based on ἐμπρέπεται and do not set the scene any more than the landscapes of Homer's similes set the scene for the fighting around Troy. Other critics have detected (or perhaps intuited) a variety of emotionally relevant metaphors latent in the sensuous picture: like the moon, the girl sheds a radiance over land and sea; like the night, memory of her brings peace; and so forth. A catalogue of such readings, with derisory comment, may be found in D. L. Page's *Sappho and Alcaeus*.[12] None of them, however, sounds more unlikely than Mr. Page's own suggestions that the whole passage is a casual virtuoso display and that "the simile has gone so far beyond its starting point that the girl is, for the moment, forgotten." The ancient critics liked to praise Sappho's verse for its πύκνωσις, συνέχεια, and λειότης ... τῶν ἁρμονιῶν, for its rhetorical and emotional coherence;[13] and her poetic remains tend generally to support their view. One sympathizes with Mr. Page's distaste for the undisciplined impressionism of the interpretations he criticizes, but would willingly avoid his conclusion that Sappho was capable of putting two stanzas of pure epideictic irrelevance in the middle of a short, intensely personal lyric.

Werner Jaeger has shown how purposefully and sometimes how ironically the iambic and elegiac poets of the seventh century could use Homeric allusion to delineate their own often very un-Homeric outlook.[14] When Archilochus speaks of his part in the ξιφέων πολύστονον ἔργον waged against the δεσπόται Εὐβοίης δουρικλυτοί, he is, as Jaeger suggests, "shaping his own personality by clothing it in the costume of epic phraseology." Even when he tells how he escaped the θανάτου τέλος by throwing down his shield, ἔντος ἀμώμητον, and running away, the epic diction helps define the quality of his antiheroic response by ironically evoking the very standard he has violated. The tension between the rhetorical surface and the ethical attitude implies the distance between a traditional, public moral code and a self-consciously new and individualistic one. Sappho could, on occasion, use epic diction with the same hearty and obvious irony, as in the epithalamium:

ἴψοι δὴ τὸ μέλαθρον·
ἀέρρετε τέκτονες ἄνδρες.
γάμβρος †εἰσέρχεται ἶσος† Ἄρευι,
ἄνδρος μεγάλω πόλυ μέζων,

---
[12] Page, *Sappho and Alcaeus*, p. 95.
[13] Longinus, *De sublimitate*, 10; Dionysius of Halicarnassus, *De compositione verborum*, 23.
[14] Werner Jaeger, *Paideia*, trans. Gilbert Highet (New York: Oxford University Press, 1945), vol. 1, p. 118.

[Up with the rafters! Raise them high, carpenters! The bridegroom's the equal of Ares! He's bigger than a big man][15]

where the epic hyperbole rubs against an idiomatic exaggeration. In her long simile, she aims at a subtler effect, but her elaborately Homeric epiphoneme creates the same kind of tension between matter and manner.[16] Its epic irrelevance coöperates with its epic diction to suggest, in this context of enforced separation, the almost inevitable parallel of the Homeric hero νόστου κεχρημένον ἠδὲ γυναικός; but the suggestion arises within an emotional situation that is thoroughly un-Homeric. Snell has observed that the phrase νῶν ἔχοισα embodies a conception of the mind foreign to the heroic outlook, for which νόος is still an essentially physical notion associated with specific, local functions. The possibility of spiritual reunion based on shared memories is never raised in the epic; thought remains too closely tied to immediate, concrete experience to suggest the kind of presence-in-absence that Sappho describes.[17]

The ideas implied in νῶν ἔχοισα were a particularly strong emotional reality for Sappho. Remembrance (ἄμμε νῦν . . . μέμναισ' οὐ παρεοίσαις) is one of her most poignant lyric themes.[18] With great precision and what I take to be a perceptible degree of insistence, she let this theme emerge from the ostensibly irrelevant imagery of her "Homeric" simile. The verbal parallel between φάος δ' ἐπίσχει (the moon sends her light) and νῶν ἔχοισα (the girl sends her thoughts) suggests a resemblance that goes beyond the terms of the formal comparison; both thoughts and light are being directed across the sea between Sardis and Lesbos. The resemblance is picked up again in the transition from the simile to πόλλα δὲ ζαφοίταισ', a transition which has often been called harsh, and is deliberately so; "wandering" goes so naturally with the preceding image of the *luna vaga* that one takes it for a continuation of the simile until he reaches "remembering" and finds that the image has changed abruptly, leaving the

---

[15] *Poet. Lesb. Frag.*, no. 111. The penultimate line remains an unsolved problem, but the Homeric reminiscence is there however the line is read. Demetrius observes the irony in the passage, although he does not associate it with the tone of the epithet, when he cites it as an instance of "metabole," which he calls a characteristically Sapphic figure—"when, having said something, she turns around and, so to speak, changes her mind." *De eloc.*, 148.

[16] Harvey, "Homeric epithets," p. 214, explains the epicisms in the simile by saying, "some sort of poetic convention was responsible for the concentration of these apparent clichés in certain contexts"—one of these contexts being descriptions of nature. But the Homeric tone of the passage goes a good deal deeper than the epithets and suggests an artistic purpose that cannot be explained simply by appealing to convention.

[17] Snell, *Discovery of the Mind*, pp. 66–68. To Snell's remarks one might add that, in accordance with "Zielinski's law," the narrative technique of the Homeric epic does not permit the representation of two persons in different places thinking of each other simultaneously.

[18] See Wolfgang Schadewaldt, "Zu Sappho," *Hermes*, 71 (1936), 368.

wandering moon and the restlessly wandering girl momentarily almost superimposed. The simile opens and closes with a suggestion that the moon's transit is a metaphor on νῶν ἔχοισα and that the sweep of moonlight across the sea objectifies the power of memory and fidelity to transcend physical separation. These metaphorical implications are reinforced by the moon's almost archetypal role as the confidante and helper of women in love. A scholium on the *Pharmaceutria* of Theocritus cites Pindar's *Partheneia* (fr. 104) as evidence that τῶν ἐραστῶν οἱ μὲν ἄνδρες εὔχονται παρεῖναι Ἥλιον, αἱ δὲ γυναῖκες Σελήνην, and another scholium, citing Euripides, adds, ταῖς ἔρωτι καταχομέναις τὴν Σελήνην μετακαλεῖσθαι συνῆθες.[19]

The moon was also thought to be the producer of the dew which nourished crops and flowers. On this subject Plutarch quotes a fragment of Alcman:

οἷα Διὸς Θυγάτηρ
ἔρσα τρέφει καὶ δίας Σελάνας.

[... such as are nourished by the dew, daughter of Zeus and the divine moon][20]

The effect of dew on vegetation was a traditional, thoroughly public symbol for the quickening of human emotions. When Menelaos receives his prize in the funeral games for Patroclus,

τοῖο δὲ θυμὸς
ἰάνθη ὡς εἴ τε περὶ σταχύεσσιν ἐέρση
ληίου ἀλδήσκοντος.

[... his heart was glad as the corn when it ripens with dew on the ears][21]

Pindar puts the image to the same use several times,[22] and another Sapphic fragment seems to use a heavily sensuous picture of moist, blossoming flowers to symbolize spiritual *refrigerium*. The scene is a country shrine to Aphrodite.

ἐν δ' ὕδωρ ψῦχρον κελάδει δι' ὕσδων
μαλίνων, βρόδοισι δὲ παῖς ὁ χῶρος
ἐσκίατ', αἰθυσσομένων δὲ φύλλων
κῶμα †καταγριον·†

ἐν δὲ λείμων ἱππόβοτος τέθαλε
†τωτ ... ιρρινοις† ἄνθεσιν, αἱ δ' ἆηται
μέλλιχα πνέοισιν·

---

[19] *Schol. ad Theoc.*, 2.10.
[20] Plutarch, *Quaest. Conv.*, 3.10.3.
[21] *Iliad*, 23.597.
[22] For example, *Pythian*, 5.99 and *Nemean*, 8.40.

ἔνθα δὴ σὺ στέμματ' ἔλοισα Κύπρι
χρυσίαισιν ἐν κυλίκεσσιν ἄβρως
ὀμμεμείχμενον θαλίαισι νέκταρ
οἰνοχόαισον.

[Within the grove cool water murmurs quietly through the boughs, and all the ground is shaded with roses, and sleep comes down from the quivering leaves. In it a horse-pasturing field blooms with . . . flowers, and dill breathes its honied scent. Come, Cyprian, take your garlands and fill my cup with nectar as you gracefully pour it into golden cups, mixed for the festival][23]

In Sappho's long simile these symbolic overtones, controlled by the verbal consiliences which frame the image, form a metaphorical pattern which gives the comparison a direct emotional relevance: as the moon crosses the sea and brings the revivifying dew to the flowers, so the girl's thoughts annihilate distance and bring some comfort to Atthis and Sappho.

The very Homeric surface of the metaphor's vehicle and the very un-Homeric quality of its tenor produce an ironic friction which it is hard to think Sappho was uninterested in. The effect is roughly like that which Emily Dickinson creates by beginning a lyric with Isaiah's image of the tents of heaven and then connecting it with the tents of a New England traveling carnival.[24] The contrast between the ordinary associations of the hallowed trope and the point of its private application reflects, in both cases, the tensions between the claims of a shaping intellectual tradition and those of an individual sensibility which, in Allen Tate's phrase, "exceeds the dimensions" of that tradition. Sappho was clearly aware of these tensions, and knew how to give them direct expression.

οἱ μὲν ἰππήων στρότον οἱ δὲ πέσδων
οἱ δὲ νάων φαῖσ' ἐπὶ γᾶν μέλαιναν
ἔμμεναι κάλλιστον, ἔγω δὲ κῆν' ὅτ-
τω τις ἔραται.

[Some say a cavalry corps, some say infantry, and others say that a fleet of ships is the finest thing on the dark earth, but I say it is whomever one loves.][25]

In her "Homeric" simile, the injection of a metaphorical content into a radically unmetaphorical figure of rhetoric gives a subtler emphasis to the distance between the heroic values and her own. Homer sometimes develops several revealing and delicately shaded points of resemblance

---

[23] *Poet. Lesb. Frag.*, no. 2. On "cool water" as a symbol of spiritual *refrigerium* in Sappho and elsewhere, see Griffith, "Early Greek Lyric Poetry," p. 42.
[24] "I've known a heaven like a tent."
[25] *Poet. Lesb. Frag.*, no. 16.

within one simile, but he never develops any real metaphorical complexity.[26] Erich Auerbach's account of Homeric style applies to the similes as well as to the narrative: "fully externalized description, uniform illumination, uninterrupted connection, all events in the foreground."[27] In his analogies, as in his fable, Homer tends to juxtapose the parts of a given whole on the same level of immediacy instead of superimposing them on different levels. His techniques of description, like his methods of explanation, seem to reflect a sensibility unaffected by the Heraclitian picture of a world in which "the invisible harmony is stronger than the visible one."[28] The complex poetic metaphor presupposes the rationalistic urge to view meaning as an abstract something "behind" or "underneath" the visible data, and this urge is comparatively weak in the epic.[29] The affective overtones in a Homeric simile like

> μήκων δ' ὡς ἑτέρωσε κάρη βάλεν, ἥ τ' ἐνὶ κήπῳ
> κάρπῳ βριθομένη νοτίῃσί τε εἰαρινῇσιν
> ὡς ἑτέρωσ' ἤμυσε κάρη πήληκι βαρυνθέν,

[And he let his head fall to one side like a garden poppy weighed down by its fruit and the spring rain; so he bowed his head to one side, weighed down by its helmet][30]

are enough to dispose of the quaint nineteenth-century notion that his similes have only one point of comparison. But the meanings of the simile are all about equally overt and generalized; they all arise from a rudimentary application of the pathetic fallacy to the sensuous image. The effect is different from that of Sappho's

> οἴαν τὰν ὑάκινθον ἐν ὤρεσι ποίμενες ἄνδρες
> πόσσι καταστείβοισι, χάμαι δέ τε πορφύρον ἄνθος.

---

[26] See Milman Parry, "The Traditional Metaphor in Homer," *Classical Philology*, 28 (1933), 37; and "The Homeric Metaphor as a Traditional Poetic Device," *Transactions of the American Philological Association*, 62 (1931), 24. See also R. B. Onians, *The Origins of European Thought* (Cambridge: University Press, 1954), p. 325.
[27] Erich Auerbach, *Mimesis*, trans. Willard R. Trask (Princeton: University Press, 1953), p. 23.
[28] For a comprehensive treatment of the view of style as "a syntax of consciousness," a reflection of the artist's fundamental experience of reality, see Wylie Sypher, *Four Stages of Renaissance Style* (Garden City: Anchor Books, 1955), chap. 1.
[29] For some recent discussions of the "one-layered," reified nature of Homeric reality, see Snell, *Discovery of the Mind*, p. 17 ff.; Onians, *Origins of European Thought*, chap. 1; M. I. Finley, *The World of Odysseus* (London: Chatto and Windus, 1957), p. 136 ff. There is a loose analogy between Homer's flat, opaque descriptions of nature and the planimetric figures of archaic sculpture. The archaic style, as Erwin Panofsky says, presented its subject through a schematic ordering of local detail rather than through a rational "view," and "renounced that apparent extension of the plane into depth which is required of optical naturalism." (*Meaning in the Visual Arts*, Garden City: Anchor Books, 1955, p. 58.) Similarly, Homer tends to order all parts of a scene, including its meanings, by juxtaposing them in the foreground, bringing them into direct and not always wholly "rational" interaction.
[30] *Iliad*, 8.306.

[... like the hyacinth which the shepherds trample beneath their feet in the mountains, and the flower blooms red on the ground][31]

Demetrius' observation that the phrase χάμαι δέ τε πορφύρον ἄνθος contributes nothing to the simile's meaning but simply "elevates the style" is a good measure of the difference between the two styles of comparison.[32] Demetrius, seeing that the passage is a Homeric imitation, judges it in terms of Homeric explicitness, and fails to see that the phrase is a metaphor on beauty blushing unseen but persistently and thus very relevant in an epithalamium for a girl who was late in finding a husband. Demetrius' criteria of relevance would be appropriate enough to the Homeric simile whose phraseology Sappho seems to have remembered when she wrote hers:

ὡς ...
... πίτυς βλωθρή, τήν τ' οὔρεσι τέκτονες ἄνδρες
ἐξέταμον πελέκεσσι νεήκεσι νήϊον εἶναι.

[... like a tall pine, which the shipwrights cut down with axes in the mountains to be a ship's timber][33]

Here it is the "visible harmony" which controls the sense of the comparison, and νήϊον εἶναι, having no metaphorical pattern within which to function, is indeed irrelevant, as Sappho's χάμαι δέ τε πορφύρον ἄνθος is not. In her hyacinth simile there is an implicit interaction between the parts of the sensuous image that is fundamentally alien to the epic simile, in which χάμαι would mean "on the ground," πορφύρον would mean "red," and the two would not combine to signify maidenly humility.[34] The stylistic difference is marked, and Sappho, who seems to have seen most of the differences between herself and Homer clearly enough, was presumably aware of it. In her long simile this difference reinforces the meaningful contrast between the heroic experience of separation and her own. An "invisible harmony," a subjective meaning behind the physical facts, emerges from both the description of nature and the description of absence. The image and the lyric emotion become, in Longinus' phrase for Sapphic unity, ἔν τι σῶμα—one organic whole.

[31] *Poet. Lesb. Frag.*, no. 105 (c).
[32] Demetrius, *De eloc.*, 106.
[33] *Iliad*, 13.389.
[34] For an opinion diametrically opposed to mine, see Max Treu, *Von Homer zur Lyrik*, Zetemata, no. 12 (Munich: Beck, 1955). His comment on Sappho's long simile, for example, is: "Dass in ihm ein Gleichnis in ganz unhomerischer Weise in eine selbständige Naturschilderung übergeht, ist die auffälligste Besonderheit." (p. 203).

Chapter III

THE IMAGO VOCIS IN VERGILIAN PASTORAL

THEOCRITUS' CENTRAL METAPHOR on the bucolic creative process was an uncomplicated one. Nature sings, while the shepherd listens and finds in what he hears a rather desultory stimulus to pastoral song. The metaphor is casually suggested in the opening lines of the first idyll.

> Ἀδύ τι τὸ ψιθύρισμα καὶ ἁ πίτυς αἰπόλε τήνα
> ἁ ποτὶ ταῖς παγαῖσι μελίσδεται. ἁδὺ δὲ καὶ τὺ
> συρίσδες.

[The whisper of that pine that sings by the springs is sweet, shepherd, and sweet, too, is the sound of your piping]

This picture of nature in song before a listening swain is one of the many Alexandrian pastoral motifs which Vergil recast in a slightly involuted form. At the beginning of the first eclogue, Vergil's swain *par excellence* is discovered not listening to nature's song but teaching nature to sing his.

> tu, Tityre, lentus in umbra
> formosam resonare doces Amaryllida silvas.

[At ease in the shade, Tityrus, you are teaching the woods to re-echo "fair Amyryllis"]

This preliminary reformulation of the received metaphor has a programmatic ring. Pastoral myth, one feels, was perhaps being subjected to the kind of subtly critical scrutiny that was later, in a prelude to epic myth, to cause the substitution of "tantaene caelestibus irae?" for Διὸς δ' ἐτελείετο βουλή. Certainly the conceit that nature hears the pastoral poet and by its echo answers him, occurs frequently and insistently enough in the *Eclogues* to suggest some thematic significance. There are, of course, a few reverberations in Greek pastoral, but there is none of Vergil's studied emphasis on echoes as the second part in a kind of amoeban song between man and nature. The Vergilian greenwood listens to the swain, just as it did when Pan started the practice of singing in rural surroundings.

> Maenalus argutumque nemus pinosque loquentis
> semper habet, semper pastorum audit amores
> Panaque, qui primus calamos non passus inertis.

[Maenalus always has echoing woods and speaking pines, and always listens to the shepherds' songs of love, and to Pan, who first put the idle reeds to use][1]

[1] 8.22.

[281]

It also listened to Apollo when he sang in the forest.

> omnia quae Phoebo quondam meditante beatus
> audiit Eurotas iussitque ediscere lauros.

[... all the songs that Phoebus once sang through while Eurotas listened happily and told the laurels to learn them]²

The woods are "argutae" and "loquentes" and "sonantes" because they have learned to repeat the songs of the rural gods and those of shepherds like Tityrus. Pastoral poetry is virtually defined throughout the *Eclogues* as a song sung to nature with the aim of awakening nature's echoic reply—as "une poésie à écho," to use Marie Desport's phrase.³

> ille canit; pulsae referunt ad sidera valles.

[He sings; the echoing valleys carry his song to the skies]⁴

> si quis tamen haec quoque, si quis
> captus amore leget, te nostrae, Vare, myricae,
> te nemus omne canet.

[Still, if anyone captured by love reads these songs, our myrtles, Varus, our whole wood shall sing of you]⁵

> non canimus surdis; respondent omnia silvae.

[We do not sing to deaf ears; the woods reply to every word]⁶

This dominant auditory image is closely associated with a heavy visual emphasis on forests, valleys, caves, thickets, and other natural enclosures. Roiron has shown that there is, in Vergil's use of *sono* and its compounds, a constant association between forests and human song: his *silvae* are essentially "cadres sonores" for rustic singers.⁷ His muse is *silvestris* rather than simply βουκολική because the forest is one of the natural echo chambers which his conception of the pastoral genre seems to require. When Vergil's Gallus considers the possibilities of the pastoral life, he sees himself among "rupes ... lucosque sonantes," happy with the Arcadians, who, as true pastoral singers, naturally sing to their echoing mountains, just as Corydon does in the second eclogue. Songs are badly sung outside the forest.

---

² 6.82.
³ Marie Desport, "L'Echo de la nature et la poésie dans les Bucoliques de Virgile," *Revue des Etudes Anciennes*, 43 (1941), 270. For a much expanded treatment of the Vergilian echo, see the same author's *L'Incantation virgilien: Virgile et Orphée* (Bordeaux: Delmas 1952).
⁴ 6.84.
⁵ 6.9.
⁶ 10.8.
⁷ F. X. M. J. Roiron, *Etude sur l'imagination auditive de Virgile* (Paris: Leroux, 1908), p. 483. See also A. G. Blonk, *Vergilius en het Landschap* (Groningen: Wolters, 1947), p. 210 ff.

> non tu in triviis, indocte, solebas
> stridenti miserum stipula disperdere carmen?

[Wasn't it you, my unskillful friend, who used to stand in the crossroads and spoil a poor song with your strident pipes]⁸

All successful pastoral songs require a resonant locale.

> mecum in silvis imitabere Pana canendo.

[With me in the forest you'll sing like Pan]⁹

> tantum inter densas, umbrosa cacumina, fagos
> assidue veniebat.

[He could only keep coming every day to the dense, tall, shadowy beech trees]¹⁰

> patulae recubans sub tegmine fagi
> silvestrem tenui musam meditaris avena.

[... lying beneath the cover of a spreading beech tree, you woo the forest muse on a slender reed]¹¹

> sive sub incertas Zephyris motantibus umbras
> sive antro potius succedimus.

[... whether we go to the shifting, wind-stirred shadows or whether we go into the cave]¹²

Phrases from the first eclogue: "sub tegmine fagi," "lentus in umbra," "frigus opacum," "fronde super viridi," "densas corylas," "viridi in antro," "altis de montibus umbrae," suggest the quality of the visual imagery that pervades the poems. These densely wooded, heavily shaded, mountain-locked hollows are both the background and the sounding board for pastoral song—"vocisque offensa resultat imago."

This emphasis on echoes and their forest cadres looks like something more than an unpremeditated expression of Vergil's fondness for verbal sonorities, and it has often been assigned a symbolic as well as a sensuous function. Cartault saw in it "un affaiblissement de la participation très vive de la nature des anciens poètes mythologiques, de cette action exercée aux temps primitifs sur les choses inanimées par la poésie."¹³ Marie Desport calls the echo of the *Eclogues* "la première manifestation, la signe perceptible à tous, d'une immense sympathie de la nature et de la poésie, du pouvoir que le poète doit exercer sur la nature."¹⁴ These suggestions that Vergil's elaborate auditory imagery defines his concep-

---
⁸ 3.26.
⁹ 2.31.
¹⁰ 2.3.
¹¹ 1.1.
¹² 5.5.
¹³ A. Cartault, *Etude sur les Bucoliques de Virgile* (Paris: Colin, 1897), p. 381.
¹⁴ Desport, "L'Echo de la nature," p. 297.

tion of the pastoral genre seem intrinsically probable and are consistent with his interest in the thematic values of natural imagery in the *Georgics* and the *Aeneid*.[15] But the Vergilian shepherd is not only a κηλέστης who, like Linus and Orpheus, fascinates nature with his song. He is also a creator who, like Sir Philip Sidney's poet, "doth grow in effect a second nature." When, for example, Lycidas hears of the near escape of Menalcas and asks,

> heu, tua nobis
> paene simul tecum solacia rapta, Menalca?
> quis caneret Nymphas? quis humum florentibus herbis
> spargeret aut viridi fontis induceret umbra?
> vel quae sublegi tacitus tibi carmina nuper . . .?

[Alas, was the solace of your songs almost taken from us along with yourself, Menalcas? Who would sing of the Nymphs? Who would scatter flowering herbs on the ground or surround the springs with green shade? Or those songs I secretly picked up from you a short while ago][16]

the reference to springs and green shade, as the surrounding lines make clear, describes one function of the poetry written by a bucolic maestro who is obviously Vergil himself. The ninth eclogue draws heavily, both in plan and detail, from the *Thalysia* of Theocritus, and it seems likely that Vergil was thinking here (as he was when he wrote "spargite humum floribus, inducite fontibus umbras" in the sixth) of that poem's picture of the Spring of Burina and its green shade, the work of a legendary hero who did not merely fascinate the landscape but who made his own.

> ἀπὸ Κλυτίας τε καὶ αὐτῶ
> Χάλκωνος, Βούριναν ὃς ἐκ ποδὸς ἄνυε κράναν
> εὖ ἐνερεισάμενος πέτρᾳ γόνυ, ταὶ δὲ παρ' αὐτὰν
> αἴγειροι πτελέαι τε ἐΰσκιον ἄλσος ὕφαινον
> χλωροῖσιν πετάλοισι κατηρεφέες κομόωσαι.

[. . . from Clytia and from Chalcon himself, who pressed his knee firmly against a rock and brought forth at his feet the Spring of Burina, and the poplars and elms wove a shady grove about it, overshadowing it with green leaves][17]

In the ninth as elsewhere in the *Eclogues*, the pastoral poet is associated with this kind of mythical creativity, reinforcing Vergil's quite explicit insistence that his Arcadia is, in Bruno Snell's phrase, a "geistige Land-

---

[15] On this aspect of Vergil's technique in the *Aeneid*, see Viktor Pöschl, *Die Dichtkunst Virgils: Bild und Symbol in der Äneis* (Innsbruck: Rohrer, 1950), and Bernard M. W. Knox, "The Serpent and the Flame: The Imagery of the Second Book of the Aeneid," *American Journal of Philology*, 71 (1950), 381; and for the Georgics, see Smith Palmer Bovie, "The Imagery of Ascent-Descent in Vergil's Georgics," *American Journal of Philology*, 78 (1957), 337.

[16] 9.19.

[17] Idyll 7.8.

schaft,"[18] that he is not merely controlling the world of fact through his poetry but is creating a second world with its own values, truth, and logic. His picture of the bucolic singer is a characteristically hazy synthesis of κηλέστης and demiurge, and the echo-filled atmosphere supports this picture in terms of a conception which, like many things in the *Eclogues*, was inspired by Lucretius.

The Lucretian *locus* on echoes occurs in the fourth book of the *De rerum natura*.

> pars solidis adlisa locis reiecta sonorem
> reddit et interdum frustratur imagine verbi.
> quae bene cum videas, rationem reddere possis
> tute tibi atque aliis quo pacto per loca sola
> saxa paris formas verborum ex ordine reddant,
> palantis comites cum montis inter opacos
> quaerimus et magna dispersos voce ciemus.
> sex etiam aut septem loca vidi reddere voces,
> unam cum iaceres: ita colles collibus ipsi
> verba repulsantes iterabant docta referri.
> haec loca capripedes satyros nymphasque tenere
> finitimi fingunt et faunos esse loquuntur
> quorum noctivago strepitu ludoque iocanti
> adfirmant vulgo taciturna silentia rumpi;
> chordarumque sonos fieri dulcisque querellas,
> tibia quas fundit digitis pulsata canentum;
> et genus agricolum late sentiscere, cum Pan
> pinea semiferi capitis velamina quassans
> unco saepe labro calamos percurrit hiantis,
> fistula silvestrem ne cesset fundere musam.
> cetera de genere hoc monstra ac portenta loquuntur
> ne loca deserta ab divis quoque forte putentur
> sola tenere. ideo iactant miracula dictis
> aut aliqua ratione alia ducuntur, ut omne
> humanum genus est avidum nimis auricularum.

[A part of the voice hits a solid place and, being thrown back, makes a sound and creates an illusion by imitating a word. When you understand this, you can explain to yourself and others how in solitary regions rocks throw back replicas of words in due order, as we seek our companions wandering among the dark mountains and call after them with a loud voice as they are scattered here and there. I have seen places that would repeat six or seven times a word uttered but once, for the hills would by themselves push it to other hills, and would thus keep on repeating words trained to return. It is such places as these that are rumored to be the haunts of goat-footed satyrs and fauns whose noisy, nocturnal revels often, according to local legends, break the silences. And they say that the sound of strings is heard and the plaintive melodies the pipe pours forth when touched by the players' fingers, and that the

---

[18] A "spiritual landscape" in T. G. Rosenmeyer's translation of Snell's essay in *The Discovery of the Mind* (Cambridge, Mass.: Harvard University Press, 1953), p. 281.

country folk hear it far and wide, when Pan, tossing the piny wreath on his half-wild head, runs over the open reeds with curling lip, so that the pipe does not cease to pour out woodland music. They speak of all the other wonders and portents of this sort, lest they be thought to live in solitary places deserted by gods as well as men. And so they exchange stories of miracles, or else they are inspired by some other motive, just as mankind as a whole is too eager to gain attention]¹⁹

Phrases, images, and ideas from this passage are scattered throughout the *Eclogues*. Vergil's opening statement of the echo motif, "formosam resonare doces Amaryllida silvas," alludes to "verba ... docta referri," and most of the reprises are colored by his memory of the scene. It clearly excited his imagination, and his special concern with it suggests that he may have seen in it not just another evocative vignette but an intriguing approach to the perennial problem of Roman Epicureanism: how to gain a satisfying hold on the intellectually exploded but emotionally compelling *veteris mendacia famae*. One gathers that Vergil was never particularly sympathetic to the ordinary Lucretian technique of juxtaposing mythical *topoi* with palinodes appealing to the *vera ratio* or holding up purple patches from legend as examples of what not to believe. In the *Eclogues* he was clearly exploring methods of measuring myth against the bleaker realities of contemporary thought without resorting to such crude disclaimers as the *Aetna* poet's,

> debita carminibus libertas ista, sed omnis
> in vero mihi cura.
>
> [Such licenses as these are the province of poets; my business is with the truth]²⁰

In Lucretius' critical but poignant etiology of the *silvestris musa*, he appears to have seen a device for suggesting to an Epicurean literary coterie that his picture of the rural gods and a sentient, sympathetic nature was a thoroughly conscious escape from a correct but slightly chilly conception of the way things are. The country folk's efforts to make their "loca sola" a little less desolate by personifying the reflex of their own voices is surely among Lucretius' most subtly ironic illustrations of *ignorantia causarum*. To these folk, echoes have become the voice of a numinous nature inhabited by homely gods and endowed with potentialities for animistic benevolence. But to the philosopher, aware of the physics of the phenomenon, these echoes are only the product of the rustics' own material *flatus vocis*. Instead of harshly contrasting myth with reality, Lucretius comes within a recognizable distance of using myth as a symbol of reality—a symbol of man's anxious search for the

---

[19] *De rerum natura*, 4.570.
[20] *Aetna*, line 91.

false but comforting stories, traditions, and world-views "quae belle tangere possint aures." The rural echo, to compare great things to small, reminds us that man's visions of a purposive universe and a pantheon that presides over human destiny have nothing to do with the facts; these visions are merely the projection of his own desires onto the facts. The teleological consolation that men like to imagine they hear the universe intimating to them is, like the countryman's echo, only the sound of their own voices.

That the Augustan bucolic poets were alive to the tonal possibilities in a mixture of Epicurean science and Alexandrian *l'art pour l'art* is suggested by the mordant atomistic *adynaton* of the *Dirae*.

> Dulcia amara prius fient et mollia dura,
> candida nigra oculi cernent et dextera laeva,
> migrabunt casus aliena in corpora rerum,
> quam tua de nostris emigret cura medullis.
> quamvis ignis eris, quamvis aqua, semper amabo.

[Sweet will turn bitter, and soft turn hard, white will seem black, and right seem left, and the structure of one substance will migrate to another before my thoughts of you leave my breast. Though you turn to fire, or turn to water, I will always love you]

The irony is, *mutatis mutandis*, rather like that produced by Day Lewis' compound of Marlovian pastoral and Marxian proletarianism in

> Come live with me and be my love
> And we will all the pleasures prove
> Of peace and plenty, bed and board,
> That chance employment may afford.

Vergil was not interested in this kind of effect, but Lucretian allusions are among his many ways of bringing into the *Eclogues* what Paratore calls their fundamental "gioco di contrasto fra realtà e sogno, fra verità e fantasia."[21] When Vergil's Silenus sings the official Lucretian account of creation to a group of fauns and naiads, one doubts if the poet expected Siro to miss the whimsey of letting the *dei indigeni* discuss a cosmology which had conclusively demonstrated their own nonexistence. In much the same way, the pervasive echo helps Vergil to hint at the insubstantiality of his rural pageant, inserting a "si credere dignum est" into pastoral myth in a way that an Epicurean circle might recognize as both *molle* and *facetum*. It has often been remarked that Vergil, unlike Theocritus, does not assume his pastoral role only as an actor within a poem. He is careful to separate himself from any of his possible *personae* and

---

[21] Ettore Paratore, *Virgilio*, 2nd ed. (Florence: Sansoni, 1954), p. 108.

to insist that Vergil the Roman poet, the friend of Pollio and Varus, is a shepherd even before he steps into the world of pastoral and becomes Menalcas. The author of the *Eclogues* claims to live in the forests, tend sheep, plait baskets, and, of course, listen to the echoes which his songs awaken. He knows that this poetry is a "poésie à écho," founded on a conscious choice of nonexistent *deos agrestis* over existent *causas rerum*. This is the choice explicitly made in the second book of the *Georgics*, where pastoral myth is held out as a refuge for weaker spirits who, like the poet, are frightened by the vast silences of Epicurean space.[22] The echo-filled atmosphere helps to inform the *Eclogues* with the basic admission that the pastoral world is a green thought in a green shade, the product of a special sensibility which has consciously excluded the world of fact.

The arrangement of the *Eclogues* is designed to suggest something less than a final commitment to Arcadia's *dolce far niente*. The subject matter and tone of the last two pieces implicitly show a poet "egrediens silvis," admitting with a typical lack of emphasis the limitations of his "studium ignobilis oti." The ninth and tenth eclogues furnish a clear thematic contrast to the first and second. The overtones of brutality and intrigue in the ninth are (whatever their biographical relevance may be) in marked contrast to the vaguely impervious *otium* of Tityrus and the bittersweet resignation of Meliboeus in the first. The element of harsh reality in this treatment of the dispossession motif refuses to be softened or transformed by a mere attitude. In the tenth, Gallus' "solliciti amores" bring into Arcadia an elegiac despair which will not yield to easy solutions like Corydon's "invenies alium." Moeris' "omnia fert aetas" and Gallus' "omnia vincit amor" both admit an imperative larger than pastoral *otium*. They introduce the emotional and political reality which Arcadia cannot stand very much of. The echo metaphor follows and reinforces this development; "the pattern of the metaphor," as Bernard Knox says of a thematic analogy in the *Aeneid*, "runs parallel to the pattern of events."[23] The tenth's final lines,

> surgamus: solet esse gravis cantantibus umbra,
> iuniperi gravis umbra, nocent et frugibus umbrae,

[Let us arise. The shade is often harmful to singers. The shade of the juniper is harmful. Shade harms the crops too][24]

remind us of the shade which envelops the first eclogue, but with a difference. The songs of shepherds like Tityrus are by definition sung in the

---
[22] *Georgics*, 2.475.
[23] Knox, "The Serpent and the Flame," p. 381.
[24] 10.75.

shade (Propertius' epithet for Vergilian pastoral was "umbrosus"),[25] and it is obviously no accident that the "extremus labor" ends with the observation that a singer can sit in the shade too long for his own good. One recalls a later and more explicit reference to rising from the ground in the *Georgics*.

> temptanda via est, qua me quoque possim
> tollere humo.

[I must try a way by which I too may raise myself from the ground][26]

An anti-Arcadian statement like "omnia vincit amor" has its metaphorical equivalent in "rursus, concedite, silvae." The tone of the tenth is precisely "nous n'irons plus aux bois," and the laurels have, in a manner of speaking, already been cut down in the ninth. The *Eclogues'* first mention of death as a physical fact is significantly juxtaposed with the image of a violated "cadre sonore."

> namque sepulchrum
> incipit apparere Bianoris; hic ubi densas
> agricolae stringunt frondes, hic, Moeri, canamus.

[The tomb of Bianor is just coming into view. Here where the farmers are cutting down the thick foliage, here, Moeris, let us sing][27]

The "densas, umbrosa cacumina, fagos" of the second have become "veteres, iam fracta cacumina, fagos" in the ninth, and in this shattered sylvan locale we find the one instance of true pastoral singers addressing a silent, unresonant nature.

> et nunc omne tibi stratum silet aequor, et omnes,
> aspice, ventosi ceciderunt murmuris aurae.

[Now the whole level expanse of earth is silent, and see, the murmur of the breeze has stopped][28]

"Aequor" has been variously translated as "sea," "lake," "marsh," and "plain" by commentators who have thought its importance mainly geographical, but its precise denotation seems less important than its connotation of flatness. This is a terrain without echoes, one which "wastes" pastoral song as the *trivium* does.[29] The imagery reinforces the eclogue's general suggestion of a weakening grasp on a once vital pastoral reality.

[25] Propertius, 2.34.
[26] *Georgics*, 3.8.
[27] 9.59.
[28] 9.57.
[29] For a summary of the geographical issues, see H. J. Rose, *The Eclogues of Vergil* (Berkeley and Los Angeles: University of California Press, 1942), p. 57. For a detailed argument that "disperdere carmen" at 3.27 means to "waste" a song by singing in echoless surroundings, see Desport, *L'Incantation*, p. 37.

> saepe ego longos
> cantando puerum memini me condere soles:
> nunc oblita mihi tot carmina; vox quoque Moerim
> iam fugit ipsa.

[I can remember that as a boy I used to fill the long days with singing. Now I've forgotten all my songs. Even his voice has fled from Moeris][30]

The echo has helped Vergil insist that his *silvae* are admittedly the objectification of a poet's state of mind. As the forest perceptibly thins out and the world's hard facts begin to press more heavily on pastoral *otium*, the echo, like the other wood-notes, ends with a dying fall. The imagery faintly but unmistakably underscores the impression that the poet has seen fresh woods and pastures new beyond the circuit of the *Eclogues*.

---

[30] 9.51.

CHAPTER IV

ECHOES AND OTHER NOISES IN THE LATER PASTORAL

ONE CAN DETECT in the verse of the Neronian eclogist Calpurnius Siculus the signs of a markedly ambivalent attitude toward Vergilian pastoral. His respectful awareness that the validity of his chosen genre depended on the *Eclogues* was tempered by the feeling that they were badly suited to the taste and values of a new age. The artistic *Zeitgeist* of the 'fifties was loudly panegyrical, but the constraint of literary precedent was, as it had always been for Roman poets, very strong. As a bucolic poet who had determined to sing, if not of *proelia*, at least of *reges*, Calpurnius clearly found a problem in the fact that the begetter of Latin pastoral had insisted that shepherds did not sing about either. Vergil had himself sung unambiguously *paulo maiora* only once in the *Eclogues* and then, as Servius says, "cum excusatione"—as if this were not really his proper subject.[1] Apparently the predominance of *mera rusticitas* in the *Eclogues* had always been a critical issue, even in Vergil's lifetime and among his own circle. His many half-apologetic remarks about the inurbanity of his muse and the humbleness of his themes, lines like: "Pollio amat nostram, quamvis est rustica, musam," [Pollio loves my muse, rustic though she be][2] "non omnis arbusta iuvant humilesque myricae," [Shrubs and humble myrtles are not to everyone's taste][3] "nec te paeniteat pecoris, divine poeta," [Be not ashamed of the flock, divine poet][4] "nostra nec erubuit silvas habitare Thalia," [And my muse was not ashamed to live in the forest][5] do not, as Hubaux has pointed out, refer so much to his choice of the bucolic genre as to his fidelity (moderate enough certainly) to the realism of the Theocritean idyll, a fidelity which Pollio and Gallus would have preferred him to sacrifice in favor of a more literary, elevated, and "Roman" pastoral.[6] Calpurnius obviously shared their preference. His pastoral sequence displays a poet vacillating between a desire to associate himself with the canonical forms and formulas of the Vergilian tradition and a desire to dissociate himself from the attitudes a use of its conventions implied. In a variety of ways, some crude and some fairly subtle, he

---

[1] Servius, *In Bucol. librum, Proeemium.*
[2] *Ecl.*, 3.82.
[3] *Ecl.*, 4.2.
[4] *Ecl.*, 6.2.
[5] *Ecl.*, 10.17.
[6] Jean Hubaux, *Le réalisme dans les Bucoliques de Virgile*, Bibl. de la Faculté de Philosophie et Lettres de l'Univ. de Liège, no. 37 (Liège: Vaillant-Carmanne, 1927), p. 1.

manages to suggest, even in the act of invoking the master, that he does not much care for *arbusta* himself, and that his own pipes, though inherited from Tityrus, are the special set "qui silvas cecinerunt consule dignas."[7] His verse is, as the handbooks automatically say, full of Vergilian allusions, but the allusions are often slightly oblique and tendentious. His seventh eclogue, for example, is a kind of urban *riffacimento* of Vergil's first. Corydon, like Vergil's Tityrus, has visited Rome, but unlike him, is determined not to stay on the farm after having seen it. Calpurnius makes an initial allusion to Vergil's definitory image of Tityrus reclining "patulae . . . sub tegmine fagi" and "lentus in umbra"; his opening lines include the two famous adjectives "lentus" and "patulus" and the equally famous noun "fagus." "Lentus ab urbe venis," says Lycotas to Corydon, and hears himself described as an ignoramus,

> qui veteres fagos nova quam spectacula mavis
> cernere, quae patula iuvenis deus edit harena.

[who would rather look at these old beeches than at the new spectacles which the young god has established in the spreading arena][8]

The allusion is unmistakably there, but instead of simply reminding us of Vergil, it ironically reinforces an anti-Vergilian choice of city over forest. "Lentus" and "patula" have suffered a purposeful change of locale. The satisfactions connoted by the first have passed from the rural scene to Rome, the overtones of protective stability in the second from trees to a civic monument.

This revision of the Vergilian image is one of Calpurnius' favorite devices for insisting that his commitment to the pastoral world is a limited one, that he has accepted the sensuous vehicle of Vergil's metaphor but not the values implicit in its tenor. The device is illustrated by his careful and almost complete inversion of Vergil's auditory imagery. Forest murmurs and "cadres sonores" are almost as prevalent in his greenwood as in Vergil's, but their effect on the shepherds has been strikingly and meaningfully changed. The first poem in Calpurnius' pastoral sequence continues, in its fashion, the tradition of sonorous *incipits* in bucolic verse.

> Nondum solis equos declinis mitigat aestas,
> quamvis et madidis incumbant prela racemis,
> et spument rauco ferventia musta susurro.

[The waning summer has not yet tamed the sun's horses, although the wine presses are squeezing the juicy grapes, and the bubbling must foams with a hoarse whisper][9]

---

[7] Calp. Sic., 4.76.
[8] Calp. Sic., 7.5.
[9] Calp Sic., 1.1.

If Vergil's woods echoing "formosa . . . Amaryllis" suggest a subtle reformulation of Theocritus' ἁδὺ ψιθύρισμα, Calpurnius' "hoarse whisper" suggests a harsh contrast to it. The sounds of the Calpurnian *silvae*, like much else in them, often grate a little. His third-century imitator, Nemesianus, shows a good understanding of the connotations of this particular *raucus* when, at the beginning of his own first eclogue, he lets Timetas observe that a shepherd can sing all the better when nature keeps silent.

> Dum fiscella tibi fluviali, Tityre, iunco
> texitur et raucis immunia rura cicadis,
> incipe . . .

[While you are plaiting a basket, Tityrus, with river reeds, and while the fields are free of noisy cicadas, begin]¹⁰

The phrase "raucis . . . cicadis" recalls Vergil's second eclogue, where the cicadas' shrillness is nature's sympathetic and harmonious reinforcement of Corydon's own strident cries ("haec incondita . . . iactabat") for Alexis.

> At mecum raucis, dum tua vestigia lustro,
> sole sub ardenti resonant arbusta cicadis.

[But as I follow your footsteps, the trees resound beneath the blazing sun to the cicadas who shrill along with me]¹¹

"Ici," writes Hubaux, "les cigales chantent pour un amant malheureux; seules elles paraissent prendre part à sa douleur."¹² But for Calpurnius, as for Nemesianus, *raucus* has lost these amoeban implications, and so has the rest of Vergil's echoic vocabulary—*garrulus, argutus, sonare, respondere*, and the rest. The forest murmurs and the other sounds of nature which Vergil had named by these words are neither a stimulus nor a response to the songs of the post-Augustan swain, but simply, as their frequent association with *obest* and *obstrepit* testifies, an irritating distraction—mere noise.

> sed, ne vicini nobis sonus obstrepat amnis,
> gramina linquamus ripamque volubilis undae;
> namque sub exeso raucum mihi pumice lymphae
> respondent et obest arguti glarea rivi.

[But, lest the sound of the nearby stream annoy us, let's leave the meadow and the bank of the flowing stream. For under the worn rock the waters echo me hoarsely, and the pebbles of a babbling brook bother me]¹³

---

[10] Nemes., 1.1.
[11] *Ecl.*, 2.12.
[12] Hubaux, *Le réalisme*, p. 50.
[13] Calp. Sic., 6.62.

> dic age, sed nobis ne vento garrula pinus
> obstrepat, has ulmos potius fagosque petamus.

[Begin your song, but lest the wind in the noisy pine tree annoy us, let's make for those elms and beeches instead][14]

> iam resonant frondes; iam cantibus obstrepit arbos.

[Now the branches are resounding; now the tree spoils our song][15]

Conversely, *tacere* and its derivatives have become key terms in descriptions of the ideal setting for pastoral song.

> venimus et tacito sonitum mutavimus antro.

[Here we are; we have exchanged that noisiness for a silent cave][16]

> hic cantare libet; virides nam subicit herbas
> mollis ager lateque tacet nemus omne.

[Here's a good place to sing. The lush field has spread a carpet of green grass, and the whole grove is silent far and wide][17]

One notes the tonal contrast between "tacet nemus omne" and Vergil's "omne ... silet aequor," a phrase in which nature's silence retains some of the sinister overtones of the Theocritean σιγῇ μὲν πόντος. Vergil's greenwood hails the apotheosis of Daphnis with a universal echo. Calpurnius makes his greet Nero with dead silence—"taciturna." Of his two references to mountain echoes, one is a sarcastic depreciation of "montana iubila" (yodelling) and the other is an aspiring poet's morose reflection that an echo is, after all, a poor way of getting one's songs in circulation.

> certe mea carmina nemo
> praeter ab his scopulis ventosa remurmurat echo.

[Obviously nobody repeats my songs except the windy echo from these crags][18]

While rejecting nature's echoic response to unpremeditated pastoral song, Calpurnius (followed, as usual, by Nemesianus) seizes upon the *Eclogues*' one reference to the *littera scripta* of ordinary poetic composition and expands it into a thematic image of his own. The reference occurs at the beginning of the fifth eclogue, in which Mopsus and Menalcas respectively lament the death of Daphnis and celebrate his resurrection. Much in the poem is obscure, but there is no doubt that Menalcas (who identifies himself as the author of the second and third eclogues) is Vergil;

---
[14] Nemes., 1.30.
[15] Calp. Sic., 2.95.
[16] Calp. Sic., 6.70.
[17] Nemes., 1.32.
[18] Calp. Sic., 4.28.

and it seems likely that a friendly but pointed contrast is intended between himself and Mopsus, a younger poet with a trace of the "vates irritabile genus" and a habit of writing out his verses with studied care.

> immo haec, in viridi nuper quae cortice fagi
> carmina descripsi et modulans alterna notavi,
> experiar.

[I shall, in fact, try out these verses, which I recently carved on the bark of a green beech tree and set to music, writing out both words and notes][19]

Menalcas' reply to this,

> nos tamen haec quocumque modo tibi nostra vicissim
> dicemus, Daphnimque tuum tollemus ad astra,

[Still, we shall, somehow or other, say something of our own to requite your song, and we shall raise your Daphnis to the stars][20]

has a corrective dash of Arcadian *sprezzatura* in the "quocumque modo" and a significant double meaning in the "tollemus ad astra," which refers primarily to the apotheosis but also implies (cf. "tuum nomen ... ferent ad sidera cycni" and "voces ad sidera iactant intonsi montes") the act of making the heavens resound, of using the welkin as a cosmic "cadre sonore."[21] I suspect that there is one more reference to the pastoral *querelle* here. Mopsus, who chooses an elegiac treatment of death as a finality and who assigns an essentially heroic role to Daphnis, writes a poetry which can exist apart from forests and echoes. Menalcas, whose verses assert the final triumph of *otium* over Mopsus' sense of loss, defends the auditory imperatives of Arcadian song. Calpurnius characteristically sides with Mopsus. Against Vergil's picture of the bucolic creative ideal,

> mecum una in silvis imitabere Pana canendo,

[With me in the forests you'll sing like Pan][22]

Calpurnius sets

> et cantus viridante licet mihi condere libro.

[And I may preserve my songs on the green bark][23]

The basic function of forests in post-Vergilian pastoral is not to produce echoes but to provide a ready supply of writing material.

---

[19] *Ecl.*, 5.13.
[20] *Ecl.*, 5.50.
[21] On the "voix forte-ciel" association in Vergil, see F. X. M. J. Roiron, *Etude sur l'imagination auditive de Virgile* (Paris: Leroux, 1908), p. 578.
[22] *Ecl.*, 2.31.
[23] Calp. Sic., 4.130.

> accipe quae super haec cerasus quam cernis ad amnem
> continet, inciso servans mea carmina libro.

[Listen to what the cherry tree which you see by the river contains on that subject. It preserves my songs carved on its bark][24]

> dic age; nam cerasi tua cortice verba notabo
> et decisa feram rutilanti carmina libro.

[Say on, for I will carve your words on the bark of a cherry tree, and will cut away the songs on the reddish bark and carry them with me][25]

> sed quaenam sacra descripta est pagina fago
> quam modo nescio quis properanti falce notavit?
> aspicis ut virides etiam nunc littera rimas
> servet et arenti nondum laxet hiatu.

[But what is this writing on the holy beech? Someone has carved it recently with rapid knifestroke. See how the letters are still green on the inside, and have not yet begun to widen and dry out][26]

For Vergil, the echo was the main metaphorical link between the shepherd's rural habitat and his poetic inspiration. The sounds that the *silvae* could produce and the *trivia* could not were the precondition of pastoral song. Calpurnius devalues this auditory image as a means of insisting that bucolic verse, in his interpretation of the term, is not only independent of the rural locale but actually somewhat inhibited by it. Vergil's complex contrast between a sylvan and an extra-sylvan reality has been translated by Calpurnius into two frankly utilitarian notions. Sometimes the contrast serves as no more than a very ordinary disparagement of the country in favor of the city, a disparagement in which Vergil's richly connotative adjective *silvestris* finds its Calpurnian counterpart in *nemoralis*, a pejorative term for the crude and inurbane. The "memorales dei" inspire only a cloddish poetry, and the Neronian swains are careful to reject such inspiration.

> carmina iam dudum, non quae nemorale resultent,
> volvimus, o Meliboee.

[I have long been meditating, Meliboeus, on songs which have nothing of the woodland about them][27]

But more often Calpurnius uses the *silvae* to mean specifically the inglorious obscurity of the self-supporting poet in unfavorable contrast to the fame which patrician patronage and imperial acquaintance can provide.

---

[24] Nemes., 1.28.
[25] Calp. Sic., 3.43.
[26] Calp. Sic., 1.20.
[27] Calp. Sic., 4.5.

> tum mihi talis eris, qualis qui dulce sonantem
> Tityron e silvis dominam deduxit in urbem.

[You will be to me like the man who led the sweetly singing Tityrus from the forest into the queen of cities][28]

This was the meaning that the woods still retained for Nemesianus.

> nam sic dulce sonas, ut te placatus Apollo
> provehat et felix dominam perducat in urbem.
> iamque hic in silvis praesens tibi fama benignum
> stravit iter.

[For you sing so sweetly that Apollo, gratified, carries you forward and auspiciously guides you to the queen of cities. Already, even here in the forest, fame favors you and has spread an easy pathway][29]

The woods are important only as a stopping place on the way to the city, and these poets are not much concerned with bringing them into any relationship to their songs; they simply want to get out of them.

When Vergil's Tityrus says,

> urbem quam dicunt Romam, Meliboee, putavi
> stultus ego huic nostrae similem, quo saepe solemus
> pastores ovium teneros depellere fetus,

[I thought, Meliboeus, in my stupidity, that the city they call Rome was like this one of ours, where we shepherds always take the young offspring of our sheep][30]

he is careful to insist that he is comparing two cities, both of them outside the greenwood. Even in a panegyric, Vergil heavily mutes the inevitable reference to an extra-sylvan source of authority and value. The dependence of Tityrus' present *otium* on the realities of Roman politics is made so vague that it is impossible to discover how the imperial edict, "pascite, ut ante, boves, pueri, submittite tauros," ever grew out of his little decision to purchase his freedom after Galatea had left him. Much critical ingenuity has been applied to writing Tityrus' Roman diary and attempting to give some legal precision to his experiences, but a hazy imprecision is obviously what Vergil wants. Although, as Tityrus gratefully admits, "deus nobis haec otia fecit," the manner of making it is abstracted as far as possible from a recognizable political act and approximated as much as possible to the vaguely quotidian concerns of the *silvae*. The city has been turned into an extension of the woodland, and even the "god's" decrees are formulated in terms of livestock. The process is exactly re-

---

[28] Calp. Sic., 4.160.
[29] Nemes., 1.82.
[30] *Ecl.*, 1.19.

versed in the later eclogists. Their green world is primarily a humble foil to civic concerns; the laurels and oaks are merely instruments in the transaction of matters of real importance.

> in quibus Augustos visuraque saepe triumphos
> laurus fructificat vicinaque nascitur arbos.

[... where the laurel blooms, destined to see many Augustan triumphs, and the laurel's companion tree grows too][31]

Their careful inversion of Vergil's primary images to support this point of view shows, in its way, a kind of indirect fidelity to the Vergilian tradition. In the *Eclogues*, as in his other poetry, Vergil had succeeded in suggesting the intellectual complexities in his relation to tradition through a delicately controlled allusiveness, through personal emphases achieved within borrowed phrases, figures, and images. Calpurnius Siculus and Nemesianus, by revising the master's sylvan scene in the interest of their own more pragmatic themes, demonstrate how thorough their apprenticeship in his school has been.

[31] Calp. Sic., 4.90.

Chapter V

THE TROUBADOUR NATURE INTRODUCTION AND SOME OTHER DESCRIPTIVE TRADITIONS

THE PRINCIPAL VEHICLE for natural imagery in the troubadour lyric is the nature introduction, an opening stanza of descriptive verse based on such rudimentary analogies as

> Quant l'aura doussa s'amarzis
> e·l fuelha chai de sul verjan
> e l'auzelh chanjan lor latis,
> et ieu de sai sospir e chan
> d'Amor que·m te lassat e pres,
> qu'ieu anc no l'aic poder.

[When the soft breeze turns sharp and the leaf falls from its branch and the birds change their songs, then I too sigh and sing of Love, who holds me bound and whom I have never yet been able to overcome][1]

and

> Lo gens tems de Pascor
> ab la frescha verdor
> nos adui folh' e flor
> de diversa color,
> per que tuih amador
> son gai e chantador
> mas ieu, que plan e plor
> cui jois non a sabor.

[The fair Easter season brings back to us, along with its fresh verdure, leaves and flowers of every color; so all lovers sing gaily except myself, who complain and weep, since joy has lost its savor][2]

The possible sources of this convention, like those of every other convention in the Provençal *canso*, have been examined closely, though often rather uncritically and always inconclusively. Proponents of the three major theories of troubadour lyric origins have all claimed to feel encouraged by the prevalence of flora and fauna in the *canso*. Ganzenmüller thought that the troubadours took the nature introduction directly from the medieval Latin lyric (". . . gerade und erst recht auf Einflüsse aus der lateinischen Literatur zurückzuführen"),[3] and his view was strongly seconded by Brinkmann: "Es kann gar kein Zweifel sein, dass dem

---

[1] *Les poésies de Cercamon*, ed. Alfred Jeanroy (Paris: Champion, 1922), no. 1.
[2] *Bernart de Ventadorn, Seine Lieder*, ed. Carl Appel (Halle: Niemeyer, 1915), no. 28.
[3] W. von Ganzenmüller, *Das Naturgefühl im Mittelalter*, Beiträge zur Kulturgeschichte des Mittelalters und der Renaissance, no. 17 (Leipzig: Teubner, 1914), p. 244.

Troubadour der Natureingang von lateinischer Dichtung kam."[4] Gaston Paris called the device an inheritance from earlier Romance folk poetry ("Il s'agit tout simplement des formules consacrées par les chansons de mai"),[5] and this notion has in part survived the general wreck of the folk song theory, for F. J. E. Raby says in support of it that the nature introduction "must have come direct" from vernacular folk song.[6] Laurence Ecker felt that the troubadours borrowed their practice from the Spanish Arabs and that it was no mere coincidence that "Frühling, Gärten, Blume, und Vögel nehmen in der arabischen Liebesdichtung eine ebenso wichtige Stelle ein wie im christlichen Minnesang."[7] Lévi-Provençal maintained, with more reserve, that an "air de parenté" was suggested by the fact that there were "en occitan comme en arabe hispanique, maints petits tableaux évocateurs, dans lesquels nous voyons les fleurs s'épanouir sur leurs tiges, nous entendons les rossignols s'épuiser en trilles harmonieux . . ."[8] A. R. Nykl compiled, to the same purpose as Ecker and Lévi-Provençal, a longer catalogue of correspondences between Arabic and Provençal natural imagery: ". . . gardens and patios filled with flowers which exhale inebriating fragrance, and are covered with dew in the morning and in the evening; nightingales and other birds singing in green foliage; clear water covered with water lilies; moonlight nights, glittering stars, shadows of trees, curtains."[9]

This accumulation of rival sources has deprived the problem of much of its respectability, and new answers are obviously less needed than new and more adequate questions. All these agreeably positive and uncomplicated theories seem to repose on an incomplete picture of the troubadours' cultural heritage, and on an imperfect distinction between literary and financial indebtedness. If recent research has shown anything, it has shown that there is very little in the *canso* that came "gerade" or "tout simplement" or "direct" from anywhere. It has also shown that such commonplaces as Ecker's birds and flowers prove no more in medieval

---

[4] Hennig Brinkmann, *Entstehungsgeschichte des Minnesangs*, Deutsche Vierteljahrschrift für Literaturwissenschaft und Geistesgeschichte, no. 7 (Halle: Niemeyer, 1926), p. 52.
[5] Gaston Paris [review of Jeanroy's *Les origines de la poésie lyrique en France au Moyen Age*], *Journal des Savants* (1892), p. 424.
[6] F. J. E. Raby, *Secular Latin Poetry*, 2nd ed. (Oxford: University Press, 1957), vol. 2, p. 267.
[7] Laurence Ecker, *Arabischer, provenzalischer, und deutscher Minnesang* (Leipzig: Haupt, 1934), p. 169.
[8] E. Lévi-Provençal, *Islam et Occident* (Paris: Maisonneuve, 1948), p. 297.
[9] A. R. Nykl, *Hispano-Arabic Poetry and Its Relations with the Old Provençal Troubadours* (Baltimore: J. H. Furst, 1946), p. 272. I have not, obviously, tried to survey the extraordinary number of theories and sub-theories about the origin of the troubadour lyric. The passages cited are intended merely as illustrations of the reductive, positivistic spirit that has tended to pervade the problem, and not as an adequate sampling of scholarly opinion on the background of the nature introduction.

literature than they do elsewhere. Nykl's more specific list might, if documented, carry more weight, but his evocative synthesis rather overdraws the staid world of the troubadour nature introduction, where flowers cheer but do not often inebriate, and where moonlight nights and water lilies are exceedingly rare. The facts of the case, which have been in part obscured by preoccupied searches for a single source, are these. First, the troubadors liked to associate love with the seasons, just as Alcaeus did and as e. e. cummings still does, and no historical theories at all are required to account for this. It is hard to know what to make of Robert Briffault's inclusion of the *chanson de printemps* among the twelfth century lyric novelties that are traceable only to Arabic sources.[10] Second, although the troubadours tended to make this association in the same rather schematic way that other medieval European poets did, the troubadours and these other poets shared large parts of the same cultural tradition. These correspondences do not inevitably imply the formal imitation assumed by most proponents of the medieval Latin theory. One may, I think, legitimately marvel at Dimitri Scheludko's belief that a direct historical connection is attested by the fact that many a Provençal nature introduction "bezeichnet den Frühling mit dem Ausdruck 'neu,'" just as medieval Latin ones do.[11] Third, if the troubadours' contact with Arabic verse did influence their handling of the nature introduction, it obviously was not by furnishing them with a fund of images of birds, flowers, and green foliage to copy. It may, to be sure, have exerted some pressure on the troubadours' descriptive style by introducing them to an exotic vision of nature; but this kind of influence is hardly susceptible to what Aurelio Roncaglia has properly called "la formulazione massiccia de 'teorie' in quel senso romantico-positivistica che tanto ha pesato in queste discussioni."[12] The French Impressionists, we are told, were influenced by the Japanese print, but this does not mean that they set themselves to drawing dwarf pines and pagodas.

I take it, then, that there are no good answers to categorical questions about the origin of the troubadour nature introduction, and that searches for the direct literary antecedents of Guilhem IX's "Pos vezem de novelh florir" are as misconceived as Wilmotte's celebrated search for the source of "desuz un pin" in the *Roland*. Instead of asking where the troubadours found the motif, I shall try to describe some specific tendencies in their treatment of it, and shall inquire how far these tendencies may conceiv-

---

[10] Robert Briffault, *Les troubadours et le sentiment romanesque* (Paris: Éditions du chêne, 1945), p. 23.
[11] Dimitri Scheludko, "Beiträge zur Entstehungsgeschichte der altprovenzalischen Lyrik," *Archivum Romanicum*, 12 (1928), 88.
[12] Aurelio Roncaglia, "Laisat estar lo gazel," *Cultura Neolatina*, 9 (1949), 67.

ably have been conditioned by other medieval lyric traditions. I am interested not only in indicating the limitations of the usual genetic approach, but also in exploring the possibility of Arabic influence in the more promising terms suggested by promising recent studies on related questions of style and structure. Álvaro Galmés de Fuentes has concluded, from his study of medieval Castilian prose style, that this style was shaped by the pressure of Arabic parataxis, "y ello no porque el árabe haya determinado la aparicíon de un estilo e-e, sino en cuanto ha favorecido y ha contribuído a desarrolar una tendencia preexistente."[13] Pierre Le Gentil's research on the structure of the *villancico* has led him to a strikingly similar conclusion.

Je ne nie pas qu'il y ait eu des contacts littéraires entre l'Islam et l'Occident, mais je pense que ces contacts n'ont été suivis d'effet que dans les cas où un exemple étranger se trouvait rejoindre des traditions indigènes preéxistantes; je suis donc porté à expliquer l'élaboration de la forme zégélesque, dans l'un et l'autre domaine plutôt en fonction de ces traditions et des suggestions qu'elles pouvaient offrir spontanément, qu'en fonction d'emprunts formels, d'imitations ou de copies serviles. . . . Cela tient à ce que le lyrisme espagnole et le lyrisme islamique n'étaient complètement étrangers l'un à l'autre et avaient découverts entre eux, sur certains points précis, des analogies et des affinités ouvrant des possibilités comparables.[14]

With this more sensitive methodological approach in mind, I shall consider some similarities and differences between the troubadours' nature introductions and those of their medieval Latin, Romance, and Arabic predecessors.

The purpose of the medieval Latin nature introduction seems to have been not merely to methodize nature but to schematize it. It is not simply that the medieval Latin poet did not number the streaks of the tulip; he seems consciously to have aimed at an unorganic, almost anti-sensuous *catalogue raisonné* instead of at an image. The pictorial details of his lyrics are usually listed in a bald series joined by such correlatives as *et . . . et, nunc . . . nunc, iam . . . modo*. His vocabulary of description is almost entirely limited to a small number of conventional generic terms and abstract epithets. Verbs of perception are, with very few exceptions,

---

[13] Álvaro Galmés de Fuentes, *Influencias sintácticas y estilísticas del árabe en la prosa medieval castellana* (Madrid: Real Academia Española, 1956), p. 183.

[14] Pierre Le Gentil, *Le virelai et le vilancico: Le problème des origines arabes* (Paris: Les Belles Lettres, 1954), p. 254. Ettore Li Gotti, in *La 'Tesi Araba' sulle 'origini' della lirica romanza*, Biblioteca del Centro di Studi Filologici e Linguistici Siciliani, no. 7 (Florence: Sansoni, 1955), has also phrased the problem in terms which my own discussion aims to support: "Il problema della 'origine arabe' della lirica romanza si può considerare metodologicamente come un problema imponibile. Non si può porre cioè come problema di 'origini.' E viceversa un problema complesso, che ancora merita di essere esaminato e sviscerato, di incontri culturali e di civiltà in un clima storicamente determinato di correnti di gusto e di mode litterarie o poetico-musicali." (p. 41.)

impersonal. Birds are heard, flowers are seen, and breezes are felt; but the poet's lyric *ego* never enters the scene to hear, see, or feel them. The only personal agents to get into the introduction proper are the members of an occasional *manus iuvenum* or *chorus virginum*. The poet's own reactions to the scene are carefully kept separate from his description of it. Indeed, one of the primary effects of the Latin nature introduction seems to lie in the abrupt *chute* from a rigidly impersonal introduction to an assertively personal exposition of the poet's condition.[15] The style had settled into a hardened convention by Carolingian times. An unusually whimsical but otherwise typical specimen occurs in a piece of *Bettelpoesie* by Sedulius Scottus.

> Nunc virident segetes, nunc florent germina campi,
> nunc turgent vites, est nunc pulcherrimus annus;
> nunc pictae volucres permulcent aethera cantu,
> nunc mare, nunc tellus, nunc caeli sidera rident,
> ast nos tristificis perturbat potio sucis.

[Now the hedges are green, now the seeds of the fields are blossoming, now the vines are swelling, now is the fairest time of the year; now the gaily colored birds are charming the air with song; now the sea, the shore, and the stars of the heavens are laughing; but we are saddened by this abominable beer we drink][16]

The style was capable of finer effects than this. The exquisite *chanson de femme*, "Levis exsurgit zephyrus," written around the year 1000, some hundred and fifty years after Sedulius' complaint, has the same impersonal, paratactical introduction leading to the same abrupt transition.

> Levis exsurgit zephyrus,
> et sol procedit tepidus;
> iam terra sinus aperit,
> dulcore suo diffluit.
>
> Ver purpuratum exiit
> ornatus suos induit;
> aspergit terram floribus,
> ligna silvarum frondibus.
>
> Struunt lustra quadrupedes,
> et dulces nidos volucres;
> inter ligna florentia
> sua decantant gaudia.

---

[15] This descriptive style had, of course, antecedents in classical and late Latin poetry. Typical examples are Horace, *Carm.*, 4.12, Catullus 44, Ausonius, "Annus ab exortu cum floriparum reserat ver," and Venantius Fortunatus, "Frigore hiberni glacie constringuntur orbis."

[16] Sedulius Scottus, *Poetae Latini Aevi Carolini*, vol. 3, p. 211.

> Quod oculis dum video,
> et auribus dum audio,
> heu, pro tantis gaudiis
> tantis inflor suspiriis.

[The west wind rises softly, and the sun moves warmly; now the earth bares her bosom, and flows with her own sweetness. Crimsoned Spring comes forth and dons her ornaments; she strews the earth with flowers and the trees of the forests with foliage. The beasts make their dens and the birds their sweet nests; they sing of their joys among the blossoming boughs. When I see all this with my eyes and hear it with my ears, alas, for every joy I breathe a sigh][17]

This basic structure was used as long as the medieval Latin lyric flourished; the goliardic poems of the twelfth and thirteenth centuries still retain it. Two typical stanzas from the *Carmina Burana* illustrate the strength of the stylistic continuity within the Latin tradition.

> Mons vestitur floribus
> et sonat a volucribus;
> in silvis aves concinnunt
> dulciterque garriunt;
> nec philomena desinit,
> iacturam suam meminit.
> ridet terre facies
> colores per multiplices.
> nunc audite, virgines . . .

[The mountain is adorned with flowers and is noisy with birds; the birds sing in the woods and chatter sweetly; nor does the swallow cease to lament her wrong. The face of the earth smiles, many-colored. Now hear me, maidens][18]

> Sevit aure spiritus
> et arborum
> come fluunt penitus
> vi frigorum;
> silent cantus nemorum.
> nunc torpescit vere solo
> fervens amor pecorum;
> semper amans sequi nolo
> novas vices temporum
> bestiali more.

[The wind blows harshly, and the leaves have all dropped from the trees because of the cold's might; the songs of the birds are stilled. Now the beasts, fervent only in spring, are sluggishly unamorous. But I, the constant lover, refuse to follow the changing seasons after their fashion][19]

---

[17] *Die Cambridger Lieder*, ed. Karl Strecker (Berlin: Weidmann, 1926), no. 40.
[18] *Carmina Burana*, ed. Alfons Hilka and Otto Schumann (Heidelberg: Winter 1941), no. 82.
[19] *Carmina Burana*, no. 83.

The goliards, too, often rose above the level of these mediocre performances (as in the "De ramis cadunt folia" of the Arundel MS), but the invariable tendency of the medieval Latin lyric, from first to last and from best to worst, was to keep the poet outside the scene he described. Nature seems to be presented as a public fact rather than a personal experience, as a concept rather than a percept. The meaning of the scene is largely defined a priori in terms of a conventional contrast or comparison, and the imagery is tailored to this conceptual frame as plastic form in Romanesque architecture is subordinated to architectural cadre.[20] Nature when green meant *gaudium*, when sere, *dolor*; and the poet did not disturb these accepted meanings by intruding private insights and associations into his picture. The standard significance of his images acts as a determinative premise which contains and shapes his description.

The characteristics of Gaston Paris' hypothetical Maying "formulas" can be inferred only from relatively late *gelehrte Volksdichtung*, from the *estribots*, *kalenda mayas*, and *pastourelles* written by courtly poets and based, one hopefully assumes, on popular sources.[21] Even this indirect evidence (if evidence is not too strong a word) shows that the tendency toward a formulaic objectivity was far stronger in medieval Romance folk poetry than it was in the Latin lyric. The closest thing to a nature introduction one finds in this verse is the opening descriptive tag: "beneath a bough" ("desoubz la branche d'un verd moy"; "solo ramo verde frolido"; "a l'umbretta del bussun"), or "by the shore" ("sor rive mer"; "pela ribeira do rio"; "an su la rive del mar"). These are the terms in which extant Romance balladry deals with the nature image; and given the extreme conservatism of folk song, there is no reason to suppose that the pre-troubadour *chanson de mai* dealt with it much differently. The main effect of the introductory image seems to lie in the same kind of rapid, formally active transition from image to gesture or image to discourse that is characteristic of the narrative ballad. The evidence, then, is against Phillip S. Allen's contention that the following nature introduction "derives straight from the vernacular lyric *Volkslied*."

---

[20] On the aspect of Romanesque sculptural style which I have in mind, see Henri Focillon, *L'Art d'Occident* (Paris: Colin, 1938), p. 98 ff. Of Romanesque style he observes, "Elle est architecturale en ce sens qu'elle soumet les figures aux cadres où ils doivent prendre place. La génie de cet art est d'avoir associé la sculpture aux fonctions." The Romanesque style seems to conceive nature (much as medieval philosophy tended to conceive it) as *formalissima*, conformable to an abstract, intellectually determined pattern and deriving its meaning from this relation.

[21] The eleventh-century Spanish *jarÿas* recently published by S. M. Stern (*Les chansons mozarabes: Les vers finaux (kharjas) en espagnol dans les muwashshahas arabes et hebreux*, Palermo: Manfredi, 1953), and E. García Gómez ("Veinticuatro jarÿas romances en muwaššahas árabes," *Al-Andalus*, 17 (1952), 57) are devoid of natural imagery and offer no help on this problem.

> Ver redit optatum
> cum gaudio,
> flore decoratum
> purpureo;
> aves edunt cantus
> quam dulciter;
> revirescent nemus,
> cantus est amenus
> totaliter.

[Spring, longed-for season, returns with joy, adorned with crimson flowers. The birds sing their songs so sweetly. The woods grow green again, and song is pleasant everywhere]

"Richard M. Meyer," Allen says in support of his argument, "has brought together a suggestive list of popular phrases which indicate with certainty the sort of source we must seek for such Latin strophes."[22] But the difference between a phrase and a strophe is perhaps enough to suggest the trouble with "derives straight from." The Latin lyrics which do in fact seem to be based on folk song stick to the formulaic compression of their originals.

> Floret silva nobilis
> floribus et foliis.
> ubi est antiquus
> meus amicus?
>
> Grûnet der walt allenthalben.
> wa ist min geselle also lange?[23]

Against the background of these lyric traditions and their handling of natural imagery, there seems almost to be a programmatic significance to the phrase, "When I see," which begins the first extant nature introduction in troubadour verse.

> Pos vezem de novelh florir
> prats e vergiers reverdizir . . .

[When I see fields bloom again and orchards become green][24]

Like many features of the troubadour *canso*, the subjective tone of its nature introductions, which is present from the very beginning, is unknown in earlier medieval European verse. The imagery is ordinarily presented as something seen, heard, and felt by the poet. Even the more or less hardened formulas emphasize the personal perception and response

---
[22] Philip S. Allen, *Mediaeval Latin Lyrics* (Chicago: University of Chicago Press, 1931), p. 279.
[23] *Carmina Burana*, no. 149.
[24] *Les chansons de Guillaume IX, Duc d'Aquitaine*, ed. Alfred Jeanroy (Paris: Champion, 1927), no. 7.

so conspicuously absent from the medieval Latin and popular lyrics: "Bel m'es quan . . .," "Lancan vei . . .," "Be m'agrada . . .," "Er ai gran joi que . . .," "Be·m platz quan . . ." Nothing in medieval European lyric verse outside the troubadour tradition, even at the most basic level of diction, resembles the following stanza by Giraut de Bornelh.

> Non posc sofrir c'a la dolor
> de la den la lengua non vir
> e·l cor ab la novela flor
> lanquan vei los ramels florir
> e·lh chan son pel boschatge
> dels auzels enamoratz,
> e si tot m'estauc apensats
> ni pres per malauratge
> can vei chans e vergiers e pratz
> eu renovel e m'assolats.

[I cannot stop my tongue from turning toward a tooth when it hurts, nor my heart from turning at the sight of a new flower, when I see the branches flowering, and the love-songs of the birds fill the woods; and though I am sad and afflicted by love, when I see fields and orchards and meadows, I am restored and console myself]²⁵

But the difference goes deeper than the diction. In some troubadour verse one can discern a movement away from the public *ver-gaudium* ratio of the Latin lyric toward a more personal reading of nature's *confuses paroles*. The Provençal nature introduction sometimes shows a poet observing a scene, feeling the Wordsworthian "interaction from within and from without," and drawing his analogy from this experience. Consider the first stanza of Jaufre Rudel's famous song to his "princesse lointaine."

> Lanquan li jorn son lonc en mai
> m'es belhs dous chans d'auzelhs de lonh,
> e quan mi sui partitz de lai
> remembra·m d'un amors de lonh.
> vau de talans embronx e clis
> si que chans ni flors d'albespi
> no·m valon plus qu'yverns gelatz.

[When the days are long in May, I take delight in the sweet songs of distant birds, and when I have gone away from them, I remember a distant love. I go on my way full of desire, sad and downcast, so that neither song nor hawthorn flower is more to me than frozen winter]²⁶

This description of bird song fading in the distance and reminding the lover of his distant *domna* is not the sort of thing one finds in the puta-

---

[25] *Sämtliche Lieder des Trobadors Giraut de Bornelh*, ed. Adolf Kolsen (Halle: Niemeyer, 1940), no. 40.
[26] *Les chansons de Jaufre Rudel*, ed. Alfred Jeanroy (Paris: Champion, 1924), no. 5.

tive European sources of the *canso*. The evocative mixture of memory and desire which comprises the half-stated analogy between two kinds of vanished beauty is quite different from the traditional explicitness of

> Anni novi rediit novitas,
> hiemis cedit asperitas,
> brevis dies prolongantur,
> elementa temperantur,
> subintrante Ianuario.
> mens estu languet vario
> propter puellam quam diligo.

[The new year returns again, the harshness of winter yields; the short days are lengthening, the elements are tempered as January enters. My mind languishes with various turmoil because of the maiden I love][27]

The goliard, to use a distinction of Jacques Maritain's, is comparing one thing to another; Jaufre is trying to express one thing through another.[28] The assonances of Jaufre's first line reinforce the dominant feeling of distance almost as heavily as does Vigny's "son du cor" in echoing "au fond des bois"; and the "jorn lonc," taken up by the twice repeated "lonh," hints at associations between lengthening days and lengthening memories. The full force of the analogy includes the unstated implications of the image, and these go far beyond the conventional conceit formulated in the last two lines.

Not many troubadour nature introductions are so subtle, but even the brisker ones often contain three novelties: an organically unified image, a real sense of subjective involvement, and a metaphor that actively exceeds the limits of a bare comparison or contrast. Bernart de Ventadorn's *lauzeta* seems closer to Shelley's skylark than to any of the *pictae volucres* of the medieval Latin tradition.

> Can vei la lauzeta mover
> de joi ses alas contra·l rai
> que s'oblid'e·s laissa chazer
> per la doussour c'al cor li vai,
> ai! tan grans enveya m'en ve
> de cui qu'eu veya jauzion,
> meravilhas ai car desse
> lo cor de dezirer no·m fon.

[When I see the lark moving her wings for joy against the sun until she forgets herself and sinks because of the pleasure which goes through her heart, alas, I so envy whomever I see rejoicing that I wonder my heart does not break with desire][29]

---

[27] *Carmina Burana*, no. 78.
[28] Jacques Maritain, *Creative Intuition in the Arts and Poetry* (New York: Pantheon 1953), p. 329.
[29] *Bernart de Ventadorn, Seine Lieder*, no. 43.

This picture of fulfilled desire impressed even Dante, with his unmatched gift for the swift, active comparison. It stands in the *Paradiso* as a simile on the soul's aspiration upward to the point where aspiration ceases and sinks into consonance with God's will. The metaphorical possibilities of a precise visual image have become important to Bernart, as they were not to the goliard, who, true to the Latin tradition, saw the *alaudula* as simply another conventional index to vernal rejoicing.

> Philomena stridula
> voce modulatur,
> floridum alaudula
> tempus salutatur.[30]

For Bernart, and for many of the early troubadours, the nature introduction was not always a variation on a public descriptive *topos*. It was sometimes a means of expressing the complexities of an individual emotion.

This combination of subjectivity and metaphorical vitality, being precisely what differentiates the troubadour nature introduction from its European antecedents, seems logically to define the area within which discussion about Arabic influence may reasonably take place. Art historians have observed that the most important thing which Romanesque decorators took from the Spanish Arabs was not a collection of motifs but a style, a feeling for the picturesque and symmetrical which imposed itself even upon their most original creations.[31] The same may hold for poetry. The early troubadours were, in all likelihood, as thoroughly exposed to the descriptive style of Arabic verse as the Provençal artists were to the Arabic style of decoration. Henri Pérès has defined the characteristic emotion of the Andalusian poet as "un sentiment profond de la nature mêlé à une sorte de culte idealisé de la femme."[32] The troubadours, who were so deeply affected by the erotic part of this mélange, could hardly have missed the natural imagery with which it was so inextricably associated. But debate about the possible effects of this exposure has turned on some rather ingenuous ideas of the effects which it might be expected to have had. The arguments against Arabic influence on the troubadours' descriptions of nature have not usually been quite so naïve as the arguments for it, but neither have they been free of the assump-

---

[30] *Carmina Burana*, no. 81.

[31] See Emile Mâle, *L'Art réligieuse en France au XII*e *siècle* (Paris: Colin, 1947). See also A. J. Denomy, "Concerning the Accessibility of Arabic Influences to the Earliest Provençal Troubadours," *Mediaeval Studies*, 15 (1953), 147; and Ahmad Fikry, *L'Art romane du Puy et les influences islamiques* (Paris: Leroux, 1934).

[32] Henri Pérès, *La poésie andalouse en arabe classique au XI*e *siècle* (Paris: Maisonneuve, 1937), p. 62.

tion that "to be influenced" means "to copy." Guido Errante, for instance, argues in the following terms:

Negli Arabi, il passagio da un termine all' altro è sempre arditissimo; il paragone si forma nel senso inverso, ascendente; dai cose agli esseri animati, non vice-versa. Questo è uno dei tratti più frequenti—direi quasi s'incontra a ogni verso—e più salienti del linguaggio poetico degli Arabi: come mai nel trovatori non ce n'è traccia?[23]

The answer to this question, one supposes, is that the troubadours took (if take they did) what they wanted and could use for their own poetic purposes. It is clear that in matters of love theory and prosody their affinity with the Arabs was distinctly elective. They were influenced by features which corresponded at least vaguely to those of their own literary traditions, and to which their European sensibilities could respond. In their poetry, as in their institutions, the troubadours had some very sturdy traditions of their own. The "subtileza de paga" that touched them was of the kind that could be assimilated to what they already knew—to the "usanza antiga." The Arabs' almost perversely subtle fancy was, of course, simply not imitable, at least not by medieval European poets; and many of their conventional descriptive devices and genres presupposed an experience and a literary tradition entirely alien to that of the troubadours. It is no more likely that the troubadours would have wanted or indeed known how to borrow the techniques of the elaborately conceited *wasf* and *nawriya* than that they would have needed to borrow the birds and flowers that Ecker and Lévi-Provençal refer to.

But Andalusian descriptions of nature were not always "arditissimo." Laying aside the oriental tropes which the troubadours could hardly have been prepared to appreciate, one still finds much that might have made a direct and powerful appeal. Some information about the nature of this appeal, and about the cultural circumstances that made it possible, comes from an incident narrated by Ibn al-Kattani and preserved in the third book of Ibn Bassam's *Ad-Dahira*.

> I once attended a reception given by the Christian woman, the daughter of Sancho, king of the Basques, and wife of the tyrant Sancho, son of Garcia, son of Ferdinand (may God chill their followers!), during one of the frequent visits I made to the court of this prince in the time of the *fitna*. There were in the salon a number of Arab dancing girls who had been presented to him by Sulamin ibn al-Hakam when he was ruler of the true believers at Cordova. The Christian woman made a sign to one of these girls, and she took up a lute and sang this song:
>
>> My friends, why does the breeze come blowing as if it were
>>   mixed with perfume?

---

[23] Guido Errante, *Sulla lirica romanza delle origini* (New York: Vanni, 1943), p. 278.

> Is it because the breeze comes from the land of my friends, so
> that I think it the perfumed breath of my beloved?
> May God water the land where my beloved of the swan-like neck
> dwells, she whose memory makes fire in my heart.[34]

The theme of the Arab girl's song was one of the clichés of Andalusian lyric poetry,[35] and Ibn al-Kattani's testimony makes it reasonable to suppose that it may have furnished some of the impulse that turned the troubadours away from the immemorial style of "Zephyrus nectareo spirans it odore" to the subjective immediacy of

> Can la frej' aura venta
> deves vostre pais,
> vejaire m'es qu'eu senta
> un ven de paradis,

[When the fresh breeze blows from your country, it seems to me that I smell a wind from Paradise][36]

and

> Ab l'alen tir vas me l'aire
> qu'eu sen venir de Proensa;
> tot quant es de lai m'agensa.

[I breathe and pull in the air I feel coming from Provence; all that comes from there delights me][37]

One notes that the Provençal versions of the motif are not imitations of the Arabic. As Errante observes of troubadour natural imagery in general, there is "ben poco dalla languida sensuosità dei poeti arabo-andalusi" in them.[38] But languid sensuosity, on the whole, *nascitur non fit*. The troubadours have seen the Arabic image from the perspective of their own lyric conventions and have filtered out its verbal and emotional sinuosities—have, in short, turned it into a nature introduction, a mere rhetorical *départ*. But what they have kept (and what makes the difference) is the presentation of the image as a subjective experience.

One suspects, *pace* Errante, that a troubadour might conceivably remain unaffected by the Arabic nature lyric's "ascendant comparisons"

---

[34] This text has been widely quoted; see Pérès, *La poésie andalouse*, p. 386, and Menéndez Pidal, *Poesía árabe y poesía europea*, 4th ed. (Madrid: Espasa-Calpe, 1956), p. 21. For a detailed argument in favor of this theme's influence on the troubadours, see Aurelio Roncaglia, "Can la frej' aura venta," *Cultura Neolatina*, 12 (1952), 255.

[35] See Pérès, *La poésie andalouse*, pp. 61, 117, 227; E. García Gómez, *Poemás arábigoandaluces* (Buenos Aires: Espasa-Calpe Argentina, 1940), pp. 85, 165; Roncaglia, "Can la frej' aura venta," p. 260.

[36] *Bernart de Ventadorn, Seine Lieder*, no. 37.

[37] *Les poésies de Peire Vidal*, ed. J. Anglade (Paris: Champion, 1923), no. 29.

[38] Errante, *Sulla lirica romanza*, p. 88.

and still respond, like some modern readers, to an even more salient characteristic: its pervasive, rather romantic avoidance of the explicit analogy in favor of suggestion and nuance. In a much-admired piece by Ibn Zuhr, the full meaning of the scene emerges indirectly when a nostalgic question about the recapture of the past merges into an image of leaves swept along by a river.

> Will they ever return, the days and the nights on the river, when the breeze was as fragrant as the musk of Darin, and we were almost born again by the beauty of the scene? The thick foliage of the lovely grove cast shadows on the river, and myrtle leaves were swept along on the surface of the water, and beneath the water.[39]

Ibn Hafağa's picture of a river coursing swiftly past a deeply shaded island implicitly reinforces the poem's theme of desire and fulfillment.

> Between the Isle of Jucar and the confluence of the river's streams, at the place where our desire made us end our stroll,
> Where the jays sang on either bank, and we saw the river hastening along its course while the Jucar wrapped itself in its cloak of leaves,
> Life advanced toward us and we hastened to meet it. The thick shade brought us a delicious repose.[40]

Ibn Hisn's *bulbul* seems to insinuate himself, like Keats' nightingale, into the poet's consciousness as a symbol of beauty's poignant transience, and then to give proof to the symbolism by vanishing, leaving the poet with only a memory and a question.

> I am moved by a small dove cooing on a branch between the island and the shore;
> Throat the color of pistachio, breast azure, striped at the base of the neck, feathers on the back deep green...
> Resting on the branch of an *arak* tree as on a throne, he bends his neck toward his folded wing.
> But on seeing my tears, he stirs and stretches on the green bough.
> He spreads his wings and takes his flight, carrying my heart with him. But where?[41]

There is, to be sure, nothing remotely like this in Provençal verse. Even Lévi-Provençal's modest assertions about an "air de parenté" seem a considerable exaggeration. But my point is precisely that the troubadours did not and indeed could not imitate such passages. What they could do, and what some of them may reasonably be supposed to have done, is to have responded in a very general way to a novel, emotionally immediate treatment of natural imagery. The evidence obviously leads

---

[39] Text and translation in Nykl, *Hispano-Arabic Poetry*, p. 250.
[40] Translation in Pérès, *La poésie andalouse*, p. 156.
[41] Text and translation in *El libro de las banderas de los campeones de Ibn Sa'id al-Magribi*, ed. E. García Gómez (Madrid: Instituto de Valencia de Don Juan, 1942), pp. 11, 133.

to little more than a *non liquet*, but even this has the considerable advantage of suggesting the inadequacy of theories which explain the troubadours' practice as either passively received from native traditions or directly borrowed from foreign ones. Those scholars who have seen the troubadours' version of the nature introduction as an inheritance from learned or popular European traditions have failed to observe that the troubadours virtually transformed whatever they might have found in either of these traditions. Those who have thought the nature introduction was simply an imitation of Arabic models have ignored the plain fact that the troubadours worked, from beginning to end, within a formal pattern that was native to Europe and had no exact equivalent in Arabic verse. Their picture of nature was unlike any other they seem likely to have known. It is in line with current conclusions about other aspects of their poetry to suggest that its uniqueness may have been the result of a creative synthesis of elements from both East and West.[42]

[42] See Henri Pérès, "La poésie arabe d'Andalousie et ses relations possibles avec la poésie des Troubadours," *L'Islam et l'Occident*, Cahiers du Sud (Paris, 1947), p. 107. Pérès concludes his discussion with the just observation, "Bien des éléments ont dû jouer, autochthones ou empruntés." See also A. J. Denomy, "Courtly Love and Courtliness," *Speculum*, 28 (1953), where Father Denomy suggests that the troubadour concept of *fins amors* was "a synthesis of borrowings and adaptations made from several sources . . . a concept of love that is a union of diverse elements of varied origin." (p. 44.)

CHAPTER VI

DANTE AND THE VERACE INTENDIMENTO OF THE NATURE INTRODUCTION

IN HIS *Epistle to Can Grande*, Dante wrote that the form or method of treatment of the *Commedia* is "poetic, fictive, descriptive, digressive, transumptive, and at the same time consists in definition, division, proof, refutation, and setting forth of examples."[1] E. R. Curtius has shown that this careful antithesis between five rhetorical and five philosophical terms is part of Dante's programmatic answer to the scholastic definition of poetry as the lowest form of knowledge.[2] Dante is claiming that his poetry has as high a cognitive value as any form of knowledge; it is a discipline which combines the modes of rhetoric and those of abstract thought. This conception of poetry presumably lies behind the remarks in the *Vita Nuova* on the *verace intendimento* of poetic metaphor. In saying that a poem's figures and rhetorical colors ought to have a "real meaning," Dante can hardly be insisting, as some of his commentators appear to have supposed, simply that they ought to have a meaning. He is maintaining that they ought to have a philosophically respectable meaning—the product of the "artis assiduitas scientiarumque habitus" recommended to the poet in the *De vulgari eloquentia*.[3] Coluccio Salutati was later to assert that a poem must, by definition, contain a reasoned philosophical or theological statement beneath its surface; otherwise it is a "simplex carmen et dictamen, non poema."[4] Dante, who clearly shared this belief although he never formulated it quite so explicitly, is applying it specifically to figurative discourse. The poet, when faced with the perennial charge that he tells lies, ought to be able to show that the metaphorical texture of his verse is the vehicle for responsible thought about philosophically significant subjects. Dante, like his friend Cavalcanti, was much preoccupied with the problem of getting a richer intellectual content into the metaphorical apparatus inherited from the troubadour *canso*. The conventional tropes of the love poetry written before the invention of the *dolce stil nuovo* clearly seemed to both of them to overlie a narrowly subjective interpretation of experience. When Cavalcanti said of the *fins amors* of the courtly tradition,

---
[1] *Epistle to Can Grande*, 9.
[2] E. R. Curtius, *European Literature and Latin Middle Ages*, trans. Willard R. Trask (New York: Pantheon, 1953), p. 221.
[3] *De vulgari eloquentia*, 2. 4.
[4] Coluccio Salutati, *De laboribus Herculis*, ed. B. L. Ullmann (Zurich: Thesaurus Mundi, 1951), p. 69.

[314]

> senza natural dimostramento
> non ho talento di voler provare
> la dove posa,
>
> [I am not disposed to attempt, without a scientific demonstration, to show where it abidès][5]

he was defining an attitude toward merely "poetic" discussions of Love's abode and allied matters. He would write about them technically—indeed scientifically—or not at all. He is warning his readers, as J. E. Shaw puts it, not to "mistake any of his statements for loose expressions or fanciful metaphors."[6] For Dante, too, the task of the *rimatori* who were willing to follow the example of the ancient *poeti* was to demonstrate the conceptual strength of their own modern "mythology." They must handle the tropes and fictions received from their predecessors in such a way that they could be reduced to something more objective and publicly meaningful than a lover's personal enthusiasms and aversions.[7]

The *canzone* "Io son venuto al punto della rota" is Dante's most elaborate effort toward what might be called an intellectual validation of the troubadour nature introduction. The traditional contrast between the cold season and the warm heart, "Tot quant es gela / mas ieu non puesc frezir," was, one imagines, just the sort of metaphorical whimsey that Dante considered devoid of his particular brand of "real meaning." I am not repeating Zingarelli's odd suggestion that Dante was disturbed by the literal falsity of the conventional claim that a lover is any warmer in winter than other people.[8] The vehicle of a metaphor is always literally false, and Dante appears to have faced this fact calmly enough in all the rest of his work. What probably did disturb him was the absence of theoretical content in the metaphor's tenor. In the first stanza of the *canzone* he puts the basic contrast in a larger and completely novel perspective designed to suggest such a content.

> Io son venuto al punto della rota
> Che l'orrizonte, quando il sol si corca,
> Ci partorisce il geminato cielo,
>
> E la stella d'amor ci sta rimota
> Per lo raggio lucente che la 'nforca
> Sì di traverso che le si fa velo;

---

[5] "Donna mi pregha."
[6] J. E. Shaw, *Guido Cavalcanti's Theory of Love* (Toronto: University of Toronto Press, 1949), p. 15.
[7] The narrative at *Vita Nuova*, 24, offers a particularly clear and detailed example of Dante's efforts to shore up specific elements in the troubadours' poetic vocabulary in this way.
[8] Nicolà Zingarelli, *La vita, i tempi, e li operi di Dante*, 3rd ed. (Milan: Vallardi, 1931), p. 353. "Ma non è vero che gli amanti in inverno sieno più freddi."

E quel pianeta che conforta il gelo
Si mostra tutto a noi per lo grand' arco
Nel qual ciascun de' sette fa poca ombra;
E però non mi sgombra
Un sol pensier d'amore ond' io son carco
La mente mia, ch'è più dura che pietra
In tener forte immagine de pietra.

[I have come to the point of the wheel where the horizon, when the sun goes down, brings forth the twinned heaven, and the star of love is far away in the shining ray that catches her so crosswise as to become a veil for her, and that planet which encourages the cold shows himself to us full on the great arc from which each of the seven casts little shadow. And yet my mind does not rid itself of a single thought of love with which I am burdened—my mind, harder than stone in holding fast the image of stone]

The astronomical picture of the stanza is this: Gemini is rising on the eastern horizon at sunset; Venus is close to apogee and too near the Sun to be visible; and Saturn is in the northernmost part of the zodiac. As a description of the midwinter sky, this is Dante's version, characteristically "faticosa e forte," of such seasonal imagery as that in Peire d'Auvergne's "De josta·ls breus jorns e·ls lonc sers." But Yvonne Batard's remark about the transformation of borrowed troubadour analogies in the *Commedia* applies here too: "Le point de comparaison est changé, et la fonction de l'image avec lui."[9] Unlike Peire, Dante is less interested in climatic facts than in the astrological symbolism of the scene. As Gemini, the constellation under whose sign Dante was born, rises, the Sun, associated in the *Commedia* with prudence, "la virtù che consiglia," is setting. The planet which dominates the sphere of rightly ordered reason cannot shed its rays (the medium of its influence, according to the *Convivio*) on the sign which presides over Dante's destiny. At the same time, Venus, the planet of love, and Saturn, the planet of contemplation, are at or near the apogees of their deferents, their stations of minimum influence.[10] This disposition of the heavens is the symbolic formula for a state of mind which Dante, like Cavalcanti, analyzed repeatedly, and which the *Vita Nuova* describes in full narrative detail. There Dante tells how he had at first failed, through a defect of the intellectual virtue of prudence, to see that his beatitude could not lie in the cupidinous pleasure which he received from Beatrice's greeting but only in a disinterested contemplation of her virtues. This intellectual failure to order his appetite toward a contemplative end had produced not love

[9] Yvonne Batard, *Dante, Minerve, et Apollon, Les Images de la Divine Comédie* (Paris: Les Belles Lettres, 1955), p. 54.
[10] For the Ptolemaic celestial mechanics of the stanza, see M. A. Orr, *Dante and the Early Astronomers*, 2nd ed. (London: Wingate, 1956) p. 178 ff.

but only a morbid psychic helplessness. In the *canzone*, this voluntary dereliction of reason is charted symbolically by the malign conjunction of the planets. Here, as in the *Commedia*, sunset symbolizes the undirected or misdirected will; "quella col non poter la voglia intriga." As the sign of Dante's destiny rises into the morally perilous *notturna tenebra*, Saturn is at its weakest and Venus is both weak and hidden, symbols of the failure of the contemplative powers and the failure of love:

> ... ciel con ciel in punto sia
> Che leggiadria
> Disvia.

[Heaven is at such a point with heaven that gallantry goes astray][11]

Astronomy thus functions as it sometimes does in the *Commedia*, as an implicit and ironic corrective to a limited human response. In the eighteenth canto of the *Purgatorio*, for example, while Dante is slothfully failing to push beyond a theory of human love which Vergil has warned him is partial and inadequate, he suddenly sees

> la luna, quasi a mezza notte tarda,
> facea le stelle a noi parer più rade
> fatte com' un secchione che tutto arda.

[The moon, retarded almost to midnight, made the stars appear more thin to us, fashioned like a bucket all aflame]

Among these stars are "quelle tre facelle di che il polo di qua tutto quanto arde." They symbolize the theological virtues which are the moral and religious goal of his journey. Even when night has made further ascent impossible, they remain as signs of the perfected love which is the end of his rational aspiration. Here the moon, Dante's symbol of man's incapacity to persevere in pursuit of the highest good, has dimmed them, commenting ironically on the pilgrim's willingness to rest content with a definition of love which does not include Christian *caritas*. The "io" of the *canzone* is, in this respect, like the "io" of the *Commedia*. The despairing lover, like the pilgrim, is not the poet, whose awareness is an absolute, but a *dramatis persona* whose awareness is measured against norms provided by the whole poetic context. Using the technique he was to perfect in the *Commedia*, Dante is doing here much the same thing that Cavalcanti does more directly in "Poi che di doglia": writing a dramatic monologue which shows sensual love as a failure of reason. "Dirò com' ho perduto ogni valore," says Cavalcanti explicitly. Dante says it implicitly through the symbolic associations of the imagery. The first

---

[11] "Poscia ch' Amore del tutto m'ha lasciato."

stanza develops an ironic interaction between the lover's conventional complaint about his condition and the implications of a scene which defines that condition from a higher and, to him, inaccessible point of view.

In this symbolic context, the conceit that his thoughts about his lady's hardness of heart have made his own mind "più dura che pietra" assumes a more sinister significance. The imagery suggests another metaphorical application of *pietra*, one which Dante, quoting Aquinas, spelled out in the *Convivio*: "color che non hanno vita ragionevole alcuna sono come quasi pietri."[12] In dozens of instances *pietra* is simply Dante's specification for a *cosa grave inanimata*—the "thing" to which he compared himself in the *Vita Nuova* because of his stultifying inability to see beyond the bare fact of Beatrice's rebuke to its spiritual meaning. Cavalcanti seems to have had the same idea in his sonnet "Tu m'hai si piena":

> Io vo come colui ch'è fuor di vita,
> che pare a chi lo sguarda, ched il sia
> fatto di rame o di pietra o di legno.

[I am like a man devoid of life, who seems, when one looks at him, to be made of a branch, or of stone, or wood]

The phrase "più dura che pietra" describes the lover's condition better than he knows. His "nature introduction" betrays a good specimen of Hugh of St. Victor's "stultus et animalis homo," the spiritual illiterate who can inspect the sensuous surfaces of phenomena without being able to determine their real meaning.

The whole sensible world is like a book written by the hand of God, which is to say, created by divine power, and the individual creatures are like so many characters—characters not arbitrarily devised by human will but instituted by divine will to manifest the wisdom of the invisible things of God. Consider the case of an illiterate man who looks at an open book and sees the characters but does not recognize them as letters; such is the case of the stupid and brutish man who cannot see what is contained within God's creatures. He sees the outer appearances; he does not grasp their inner meaning.[13]

The imagery of the rest of the *canzone* explores this dimension of the *pietra* metaphor, as the lover describes a profoundly relevant page of God's book but sees only its material configurations and, in his self-absorption, misses all its meaning for him. The natural imagery of the analogy is like that of the similes in the *Inferno*, which often contain, along with visible meanings which the pilgrim can understand, clues to

---

[12] *Convivio*, 2.1.
[13] Hugh of St. Victor, *Eruditionis didascalicae liber septimus*, Patrologia Latina, no. 176, col. 814.

deeper meanings which, as Irma Brandeis says, "because they could not be read by the pilgrim when he saw them, Dante transcribes without stress, hidden in the apparently sufficient concrete comparison."[14]

The second and fifth stanzas (which frame the third and fourth as part of a larger symmetry) are dominated by images of elemental rise and fall. With close structural parallelism, they emphasize winter's power to turn ascent into descent. In the second stanza, the hot, rising African wind passes the Mediterranean to become a cloud-laden pall over Europe, and then falls in a mass of snow and rain.

> Levasi della rena d'Etiopia
> Lo vento peregrin, che l'aer turba,
> Per la spera del sol ch'or la rescalda;
>
> E passa il mare, onde n'adduce copia
> Di nebbia tal che, s'altro non la sturba,
> Questo emispero chiude tutto, e salda;
>
> E poi si solve, e cade in bianca falda
> Di fredda neve, ed in noiosa piaggia;
> Onde l'aere s'attrista tutto, e piagne.
> Ed amor, che sue ragne
> Ritira al ciel per lo vento che poggia,
> Non m'abbandona, sì è bella donna
> Questa crudel, che m'è datta per donna.

[From the sand of Ethiopia rises the foreign wind which troubles the air because of the sphere of the sun which now burns it; and it passes the sea, from which it brings us a mass of clouds so that, unless another wind hinders it, it closes and seals up this whole hemisphere; and then it dissolves and falls in white flakes of cold snow and in grievous rain, at which the air is all saddened and weeps. And Love, who pulls his nets down from the sky because of the battering wind, does not abandon me, so fair a lady is this cruel one who is given me for lady]

The cycle is repeated in the fifth stanza as the warm waters which are drawn up from within the earth become a sluggish river and finally an unmoving sheet of ice.

> Versan le vene le fumifere acque
> Per li vapor che la terra ha nel ventre,
> Che d'abisso gli tira suso in alto;
>
> Onde cammino al bel giorno mi piacque,
> Che ora è fatto rivo, e sarà, mentre
> Che durerà del verno il grande assalto

---

[14] Irma Brandeis, "Metaphor in the Divine Comedy," *Hudson Review*, 8 (1955), 558.

> La terra fa un suol che par di smalto,
> E l'acqua morta si converte in vetro
> Per la freddura che di fuor la serra.
> Ed io della mia guerra
> Non son però tornato un passo arreto,
> Nè vo tornar; chè se 'l martiro è dolce,
> La morte de' passare ogni altro dolce.

[The springs pour forth their steaming waters, because of the vapor which the earth has within her womb, which draws them upward from the abyss; and so the road which pleased me in fair weather has now been made a river and will be while the great assault of winter lasts. The earth makes a surface which seems cemented, and the stagnant water turns to glass because of the cold which grips it from without. And I have not, for all that, drawn back one step from my war, nor shall I, for if martyrdom is sweet, death must surpass all other sweetness]

One detects here an application of the fundamental analogy between gravitational motion and *moto spiritale* upon which Dante, "le plus verticalisant des poètes,"[15] founded the whole structure of the *Commedia* and which he made the theme of dozens of comparisons like,

> Poi come il foco movesi in altura,
>   per la sua forma, ch'è nata a salire
>   là dove più in sua materia dura,
>
> così l'animo preso entra in disire

[Then, as fire moves upward because of its form, which is born to rise to the point where it endures longest in its material, so the enamored soul enters into desire][16]

and,

> Così da questo corso si diparte
>   talor la creatura, ch' ha potere
>   di piegar, così pinta, in altre parte
>
> (e sì come veder si può cadere
>   foco di nube), se l'impeto primo
>   a terra è torto da falso piacere.
>
> Non dei ammirar, se bene estimo,
>   lo tuo salir, se non come d'un rivo
>   se d'altro monte scende ad imo.

[Thus the creature sometimes departs from this course because it has power, when thus impelled, to swerve in another direction (just as fire can be seen to fall from a cloud), if its initial impetus is turned aside to earth by false pleasure][17]

All these images, so central to Dante's thought, are based on the Augustinian concept of a *pondus amoris*, an appetitive gravitational system which embraced all orders of creation. In the *De civitate Dei* Augustine

---

[15] Gaston Bachelard, *L'Air et les songes* (Paris: Corti, 1943), p. 51.
[16] *Purg.*, 18.28.
[17] *Parad.*, 1.130.

wrote, "If we were stones or waves or winds or fire or the like, without any sensory perception at all, still we should not lack a certain urge toward our own place in the order of things. For the directions taken by material objects are like the loves of animate bodies, whether they proceed downward because of heaviness or upward because of lightness."[18] And in the thirteenth book of the *Confessions*, in a passage on the Holy Spirit to which Dante was much indebted in other ways, he wrote, "A material object moves toward its own place through its weight, not necessarily downward but toward its own place. Fire moves upward, a stone moves downward ... My weight is my love; by it I am borne wherever I am borne."[19] The natural direction of the free will is upward; when distorted and encumbered by unnatural desire it moves downward. The hot wind and the steaming waters, whose light ascent winter has turned into an earthseeking heaviness, symbolically trace the trajectory of a soul deflected by *falso piacere* from its true goal. This is the spiritual state that seems to be described in Dante's curious first letter to the Marquis Moruello Malaspina di Giovagallo, which is presumably connected with the *canzone*: "Amor, dacchè convien pur ch'io doglia." I do not claim to know what the intention of the letter was, but I feel comparatively certain that Dante was not, at this stage in his life, using phrases like "liberum meum ligavit arbitrium" without having their technical implications in mind. ". . . and finally, that my soul might never again rebel against him, Love bound my free will, so that I must turn not where I desire, but where he desires. Therefore Love reigns within me, since there is no power there to oppose him, and how he rules me you must inquire outside these presents."[20] Some of the later *canzoni* do in fact show "qualiter me regnat" with a theoretical exactitude that has not always been appreciated.

Framed by this picture of physical and psychic descent, the third and fourth stanzas describe another kind of seasonal response. Within a scene that ironically demonstrates the lover's spiritual condition, there are clear signs that the condition is not ineluctable. The road up the mountain can be seen even from the depth of the dark wood.

> Fuggito è ogni augel che 'l caldo segue
> Dal paese d'Europa, che non perde
> Le sette stelle gelide unquemai;

---

[18] *De civitate Dei*, 11.28.
[19] *Confessions*, 13.9. This text and the preceding one are cited and discussed by Guido Manacorda, *Poesia e contemplazione* (Florence: Sansoni, 1947), p. 157 ff.
[20] ". . . et denique, ne contra se amplius anima rebellaret, liberum meum ligavit arbitrium, ut non quo ego, sed quo ille vult, me verti oportet. Regnat itaque Amor in me, nulla refragante virtute; qualiter me regnat, inferius extra sinum praesentium requiratis."

E gli altri han posto alle lor voce triegue
   Per non sonarle infino al tempo verde,
   Se ciò non fosse per cagion di guai;

E tutti gli animali che son gai
   Da lor natura son d'amor disciolti,
   Perrochè il freddo lo spirito gli ha ammorta.
E 'l mio più d'amor porta,
   Chè gli dolci pensier non mi son tolti,
   Nè mi son dati per volta di tempo;
   Ma donna gli mi da di picciol tempo.

Passato hanno lor termine le fronde
   Che trasse fuor la virtù del Ariete
   Per adornare il mondo, e morta è l'erba;

Ramo di foglia verde non s'asconde,
   Se non in lauro, in pino, od in abete,
   Od in alcun che sua verdura serba;

E tanto è la stagion forte ed acerba,
   Ch'ha morti gli fioretti per le piagge,
   Gli quai non posson tollerar la brina.
E la crudele spina
Amor però di cor non la mi tragge;
Ond'io son certo de portarla sempre
Ch'io sarò in vita, s'io vivessi sempre.

[Every bird which follows the warmth has fled from the region of Europe, which never loses the seven cold stars, and the others have set a truce upon their voices, not to sound them until the green season, unless it be for the sake of wailing. And all the animals that are by nature amorous are loosed from love because the cold has killed their spirit. And mine bears more love because my sweet thoughts are neither taken from me nor given to me by the change of the seasons, but a lady of short season gives them to me.

The leaves which the strength of Aries drew forth to adorn the world have passed their limit, and the grass is dead. No branch hides itself in green foliage except the laurel, the pine, or the fir, or any other that keeps its verdure. And so strong and harsh is the season that it has killed the flowers on the hills, those which cannot endure the frost. And Love, for all that, does not draw the cruel thorn from my heart, and so I am sure to bear it as long as I live, if I live forever]

The two stanzas are paired as precisely as the two which frame them. The migratory birds have flown to warmer climates, the other birds remain silent and miserable in the cold, and the warm-blooded animals have sunk into a deathlike torpor. Similarly, the evergreen trees have kept their foliage, the deciduous trees have withered, and the grass and flowers are dead. In the birds of passage and the evergreens, Dante has chosen two of the commonest medieval symbols for prudence and contemplation, the virtues countervalent to the particular aberrancy of the will described in the first stanza. In his tropological discussion of the swallow, Hugh of St. Victor interprets its southerly flight as a symbol of prudent withdrawal from the occasions of concupiscence: "When the winter of cupidity comes on and its chill increases, then the righteous man crosses over to the warmth of charity and patiently waits there until the chill of temptation leaves his mind."[21] The contrast between the evergreen leaves and the flowers and grass, typifying the contrast between the enduring virtues of contemplation and the transitory delights of the active life, had a long history before and after Dante.[22] In his *Breviari d'Amor*, Matfré Ermengaud wrote of the flowers and leaves on his diagramed *arbre d'amor*,

> Et en las flors eschrichas so
> las vertutz d'operatio...
> mas las vertutz e·ls aips per quals
> tots homs se garda de far mals...
> e son de contemplatio
> pro mais que d'operatio
> son en las fuelhas pausadas.

[And on the flowers are inscribed the operative virtues, but the virtues and qualities through which all men refrain from doing evil, and those of contemplation rather than operation are placed on the leaves][23]

And as Eustache Deschamps observed in one of his *ballades* in praise of the Order of the Leaf, which opposed the Order of the Flower by maintaining that a lover should give more attention to the reflective, cautionary virtues,

> Et s'il avaient qu'il face un po de vent,
> la fleur verrez et sa couleur palir,
> en ordure chiet et vau au neant,
> fruit et couleur il faut perdre et perir;
> maiz la fueille ne puet nul temps morir;
> toujour se tient forte, ferme, et loyaulx.

[And if a little wind occurs, you will see the flower's color become pale; it falls into ordure and comes to nothing; it must lose its fruit and color, and perish. But the leaf can never die; it keeps itself strong, firm, and loyal][24]

The imagery of the ode's two central stanzas symbolically recommends prudence and contemplation, the virtues whose failure has been represented in the other stanzas, as defences against a spiritual winter and the

---

[21] Hugh of St. Victor, *De bestiis*, Patrologia Latina, vol. 177, col. 43.
[22] On the history of this allegorical motif in French and English literature, see George L. Marsh, "Sources and Analogues of the Flower and the Leaf," *Modern Philology*, 4 (1906), 121, 281.
[23] Matfré Ermengaud, *Le Breviari d'Amor*, ed. Gabriel Azaïs (Paris, 1862–1881), lines 450 ff.
[24] This text and others connected with it may be found in Marsh, "Sources and Analogues," p. 286 f.

kind of death it can bring. The complaint of a man enmeshed in the sensual passion which Dante had once analyzed and renounced is here presented dramatically against a natural background which, like the pavement of Purgatory, mutely describes both the condition and the remedies of sin.

One ought perhaps to say of the *tornato*, "l'ultimo verso per la litterale espositione assai legermente qua si può ridurre." But the poem's whole symbolic fabric focuses attention on a final irony.

> Canzone, or che sarà di me nell' altro
> Dolce tempo novello, quando piove
> Amore in terra da tutti li cieli,
> Quando per questi geli
> Amore è solo in me, e non altrove?
> Sarà di me quel ch'è d'un uom di marmo
> Se in pargoletta fia per cuore un marmo.

[My ode, what will become of me in the next sweet new season, when love rains on the earth from all the heavens, if during these frosts love is in me and nowhere else? I shall become what a man of marble is, if in the maiden there is marble for a heart]

Just as winter was a standard medieval symbol for cupidinous mortality, so the springtime was a metaphorical commonplace for another *innovatio mundi*, the Last Day. By his sentimental cliché that in Spring love will rain down from all the heavens, the lover directs our attention away from the *ver brevis*, about which his cliché is technically false, toward the *longus Aprilis* of the Resurrection, about which it is true. The only "Spring" in which each of the ten heavens will, *secondo verità*, have its specific virtue subsumed under one influence will be the Last Judgment, when the planets will stand "in their habitations,"[25] thus ceasing to actualize divine providence, and the whole rational creation will feel the unmediated presence of Love. In the face of this tension between a rhetorical conceit and a latent *verace intendimento*, the question "or che sarà di me?" takes on some of the eschatological overtones of the hymn's "quis tunc ego sum dicturus?" The final couplet suggests an answer that was later to be given in the *Commedia*: the whole, hylomorphic man will participate in the condition which the soul has chosen during this life. The "mente ch'e più dura che pietra" will produce a "uom di marmo."

The fact that this *canzone*, like the rest of the *rime pietrose*, deals with the kind of sensual love which Dante, at the time of "Donne, ch'avete intelletto d'amore," had abandoned as a subject for poetry, has often

---

[25] For a discussion of this point based on Habakkuk, 3:11 ("Sol et luna steterunt in ordine suo") and Job, 26:11, see Petrus Lombardus, *Sententiarum libri quatuor*, 4. 44, 5.

been taken to mean that it must contain a *nascosa veritade* on a chaster theme. This theme has generally been identified as a disinterested passion for *Filosofia*, and Dante's importunate addresses to "Donna Pietra" have been interpreted in much the same way that he himself interpreted his rarefied praise of the *donna gentile*. Not many diaskeuasts have gone so far as Federzone, who identified the wind from Ethiopia with the philosophy of Averroes and turned the poem into a Catholic apologia.[26] But the results have always been curious. Zingarelli managed to find in Dante's description of frustrated passion the symbol of "la felicità del sapiente che non conosce turbamenti," and to interpret the whole poem in the spirit of his remarks on the *crudele spina* of the fifth stanza: "Ma bisogna pensare che la spina porta la rosa, e le sue poesie come rose adornano il mondo in cambio di foglie e fiori e fronde."[27] This tendency to let guesses about Dante's purposes substitute for a careful reading of his lyrics is always bad enough, and becomes disastrous in the later *canzoni*. Their polysemous technique is far closer to that of the heavily textured, implicitly symbolic narrative of the *Commedia* than to that of the transparent, explicitly referential allegory of the *Roman de la Rose*. Dante obviously does full justice to the literal, conventional analogies of the nature introduction, and we are not asked to ignore them in favor of abstract meanings that have no ethically or dramatically functional relation to them. There is much to be said for Cosmo's suggestion that the *rime pietrose* are the technical experiments of a transitional period in Dante's art.[28] And one aspect of the experiment was surely the use of a poetic *sensus litteralis* which the reader is not expected to "reduce" to theology or philosophy but rather to see as a palpable reality, informed, like human existence itself, by larger meanings which orient and enrich it.[29]

[26] Giovanni Federzone, "La canzone di Dante, 'Io son venuto al punto della rota,' preludio alla Divina Commedia," *Giornale Dantesco*, 19 (1911), 147, 197. It is noteworthy that Luigi Valli in *Il linguaggio segreto di Dante e dei 'Fedeli d'Amore'* (Rome: L'Universale, 1928), p. 342 ff., using the same hermetic methods as Federsone, discovered that the canzone, far from being a paean to orthodoxy on the occasion of the Jubilee, was actually a manifesto of heresy and antipapalism.
[27] Zingarelli, *La vita*, p. 360.
[28] Umberto Cosmo, *A Handbook of Dante Studies*, trans. David Moore (New York: Barnes and Noble, 1947), p. 53.
[29] Dante's own statements about the kind of allegory employed in the *canzoni* have, in my opinion, been widely misunderstood. For a discussion of the relevant passages in the *Convivio*, see the Appendix (p. 329).

APPENDIX

APPENDIX

DANTE'S CANZONI AND THE "ALLEGORY OF POETS"

DANTE'S DISCUSSION OF ALLEGORY in the second book of the *Convivio* has been called confused and inconsistent almost often enough to qualify it as a *locus desperatus*. The majority opinion seems to be that Dante was trying to recapitulate a scholastic distinction between Biblical and secular semantics, and that, missing the point, he blundered into the proposition that there is no real difference between the meaning structure of Exodus and that of the *Metamorphoses*. This opinion seems to me mistaken, and I shall offer in its stead the suggestion that the passage is in the main what Dante says it is: a technically valid ex parte account of the kind of analysis which he proposes to apply to his odes.

I say that, as was told in the first chapter, this exposition must be both literal and allegorical; and that this may be understood it should be known that writing may be taken and should be expounded chiefly in four senses. The first is called the literal, and it is the one that extends no further than the letter as it stands; the second is called the allegorical and it is the one that hides itself under the mantle of these tales, and is a truth hidden under beauteous fiction. As when Ovid says that Orpheus with his lyre made wild beasts tame and made trees and rocks approach him; which would say that the wise man with the instrument of his voice makes cruel hearts tender and humble; and moveth to his will such as have not the life of science and art; for they that have not the rational life are as good as stones. And why this way of hiding was devised by the sages will be shown in the last treatise but one. It is true that the theologians take this sense otherwise than the poets do, but since it is my purpose to follow the method of the poets, I shall take the allegorical sense after the use of the poets.

The third sense is called moral, and this is the one that lecturers should go intently noting throughout the scriptures for their own behoof and that of their disciples. Thus we may note in the Gospel, when Christ ascended the mountain for the transfiguration, that of the twelve apostles he took with him but three; wherein the moral may be understood that in the most secret things we should have but few companions.

The fourth sense is called the anagogical, that is to say "above the sense"; and this is when a scripture is spiritually expounded which even in the literal sense, by the very things it signifies, signifies again some portion of the supernal things of eternal glory, as may be seen in the song of the prophet which saith that when the people of Israel came out of Egypt, Judea was made holy and free. Which although it is manifestly true according to the letter is none the less true in its spiritual intention; to wit, that when the soul goeth forth out of sin, it is made holy and free in its power.[1]

Dante's reference to a "poetic" and a "theological" allegory has usually been understood as a muddled reminiscence of the standard

---

[1] *Convivio*, 2.1, trans. Phillip H. Wicksteed (London: Dent, 1903), p. 63.

exegetical contrast between verbal signification and figural allegory—between a human semantic in which words mean things and a divine semantic in which words mean things which sacramentally mean other things.[2] A corollary of this interpretation is that Dante must have thought, when he wrote these lines, that Ovid wrote allegory in about the same way that the Holy Spirit did. To quote the most recent critique, "his lack of awareness of the metaphysical and theological presuppositions of the anagogical sense, and his generally inconsistent treatment of the question indicate that Dante assumed the structural identity of both kinds of allegory."[3] If so, Dante was badly confused about a very elementary matter, but the contrast between Biblical type and secular trope may not have been exactly what he had in mind. Certainly other contrasts were available. Coluccio Salutati was simply repeating a commonplace of *trecento* and *quattrocento* poetics when he observed that a poem of whatever kind was, after all, part of the universal economy, and was as likely as any other part to be a *signum naturale* bodying forth God's purposes independently of human intentions.

Having been written by the Holy Spirit, the Bible is directed toward an infinitude of meanings, nor can a reasonable meaning be deduced from its letter which that infinite wisdom from whose throne it proceeded in the beginning did not intend. But human poetry, being a human invention, is sometimes directed toward a meaning because it was related by God, the author of all things, to something of which the human author was not aware, and sometimes because it merely includes a meaning which the human author wished it to have.[4]

Consequently, one can interpret a *bella menzogna* in two ways. For example,

Vergil, wishing to flatter either Augustus or the Romans, made the following prophecy, and in it we can plainly see that he was telling a falsehood: *his ego nec metas rerum nec tempora pono; imperium sine fine dedi*. These were not presented as the poet's own words but as the words of a false god falsely prophesying, although it was not in fact Jove who said these words but the poet. And if, as many maintain, Vergil should be said to have prophesied something that *was* true, this was not his own intention but the intention of God. It was the strength of truth breaking out even amid a falsehood.[5]

---

[2] This view of the passage has been closely associated, during the past decade, with Professor Singleton's interesting and seminal misinterpretation of the phrase, "since it is my purpose to follow the method of the poets." In the article "Dante's Allegory," *Speculum*, 25 (1950), 78, he maintained that Dante meant by this that he was going to introduce into the prose text of the *Convivio* a "fictive abstraction," Lady Philosophy. The context of the phrase, however, makes it clear he means to show that he wrote poetic allegory in his odes, not that he is going to write it in the *Convivio*.

[3] Joseph Anthony Mazzeo, "Dante's Conception of Poetic Expression," *Romanic Review*, 47 (1955), 241.

[4] Coluccio Salutati, *De laboribus Herculis*, ed. B. L. Ullmann (Zurich: Thesaurus Mundi, 1951), p. 87.

[5] *Ibid.*, p. 14.

Salutati's poetically oriented distinction may possibly provide a better gloss on Dante's obscurities than the theologically oriented distinctions of Aquinas and Hugh of St. Victor. Dante is not thinking of the difference between scriptural and secular exegesis; he is thinking of the difference between two kinds of interpretation that are theoretically applicable to the study of all literature, sacred and profane. That is, one may interpret a work either poetically, in terms of the conscious intention of the author, or theologically, in terms of God's intention operating through the poet. By saying that he will employ the method of the poets, Dante means simply that he is going to interpret his odes, as he has just interpreted Ovid, by revealing meanings which he consciously and on principle concealed when he wrote them—without prejudice to the possibility that they might also be interpreted theologically. In the *Vita Nuova*, one recalls, Dante had reconsidered some of his earlier poetry and had discovered in it a significance which had escaped him when he wrote it, "ma ora è manifesto." He had lived through and described in his verse an experience into which God had put a profound meaning; but nobody, least of all Dante, saw it at the time. Using the method of the theologians in the *Vita Nuova*, he found the message of salvation rubbed into the grain of his early life and work in the same way that it had been rubbed into the grain of history.[6] The method of interpretation to be employed in the *Convivio* is not, he says, that kind.

What, then, about Dante's reference to "In exitu Israel"? Must one conclude, with Nardi and others who have found the passage confused,[7] that Dante simply committed a casual error in implying that the psalmist "meant" his anagoge in the same way that Ovid "meant" his allegory? Or is there a possibility that Dante understood the theoretical complexities of the problem better than some of his critics? In the opinion of Aquinas, there were men in the state of the Old Testament who were the unconscious vehicles of prophecy, and in the accounts of their words and actions one might look for the higher meanings which only God could put in them. But there were also men "who, having charity and grace of the Holy Spirit, looked chiefly to spiritual and eternal promises."[8] These men, having received inspired insight into the spiritual significance of Jewish history, could write about the events of that history conscious of their prophetic bearing. In such cases, according to Aquinas, the

---

[6] Professor Singleton has observed that Dante implicitly compares his own exegetical methods in the *Vita Nuova* with those of Augustine. See *An Essay on the Vita Nuova* (Cambridge, Mass.: Harvard University Press, 1951), p. 43.

[7] Bruno Nardi, "I sensi delle Scritture," in *Nel mondo di Dante* (Rome: Edizioni di Storia e Litteratura, 1944), p. 55.

[8] *Summa Theologica:* I–II. cvii.1.

spiritual reference is not part of the allegory but part of the letter, the letter being defined as the full intention of the human author. Stephen Langton, expounding Balaam's prophecy, "A star shall rise out of Jacob" (Num. 24:17), wrote:

> This is a manifest prophecy of Christ. Hence no literal interpretation other than the prophecy ought to be understood. Thus we should expound the letter: A star, Christ, shall rise through incarnation out of Jacob, the Jewish people ... Literally, this was fulfilled under David that it might mystically signify that Christ should strike the vices (i.e., the chiefs of Moab) and possess their lands, that is, the men whom sin has in bondage.[9]

Langton's point is that the Christological meaning of the prophet's words, because it was presumably in his mind as he uttered them, is not to be taken as figural allegory but rather as prophetic metaphor. One must distinguish between the scriptural history of David, into whose events God put a Christian significance, and the prophet's reference to David, into which the prophet put a Christian significance he had learned from God. It seems probable that Dante, in selecting for interpretation not the fact of the Exodus, nor a passage from Exodus, but "the song of the prophet" about the Exodus, had this distinction in mind. Certainly he had good precedent for treating Psalm 113 in this way. Augustine had clearly pointed out that while Exodus contains *figurae rerum*, true figural allegories, the psalm contains *figurae verborum*, metaphors based on prophetic access to the meaning of the Exodus:

> When we read in the psalm, "In exitu Israel de Aegypto, domus Jacob de populo barbaro, facta est Judaea sanctificatio eius ...," let us not suppose that history is being retold but that the future is being foretold. When this miracle happened to the Jewish people, it happened as a fact, but a fact with future significance. But the purpose of the man who prophesied through his psalmistry was to show that he was doing with words what was done in Exodus with facts. And the same Spirit caused both the facts and the words in order that the things which were to be fully manifest only at the end of the world should be announced by the concurrence of both figural history and figurative language. And so the psalmist did not remain entirely faithful to history, but departed in certain respects from the account found in Exodus, lest he should be thought to be writing about things done instead of about things to come.[10]

Dante is implying, without laboring so obvious a point, that the anagoge was intended by the psalmist, and that the psalm's spiritual reference is thus technically the tenor of a metaphor—just as Ovid's secular reference is. He is not mistakenly assuming the "structural identity" of figural

---

[9] Quoted by Beryl Smalley, *The Study of the Bible in the Middle Ages* (Oxford: Blackwell, 1952), p. 233.
[10] *Enarratio in psalmum cxiii*, Patrologia Latina, vol. 37, col. 1475.

allegory and literary personification; he is *suadente auctoritate* assuming the structural identity of two passages he has selected to illustrate his thesis.

These remarks also apply, in a somewhat different way, to the passage Dante interprets tropologically in the second paragraph. Here, of course, there is no question at all of figural meanings. The interpretation, like almost all later medieval New Testament tropology, was what some commentators called *moralitas secundum litteram*—not a "higher" meaning but a direct moral precept contained in the text. The passage means that "in the most secret things we should have but few companions" precisely because Jesus was embarking on a most secret thing and desired to have few companions. Again, one is dealing with a meaning which was presumably within the purview of the author—not perhaps a *nascosa veritade* in the fullest sense of the term, but at least an implication whose force the unskilled reader is likely to miss and which it is the business of the exegete to render explicit by earnest personal application.

Dante's point is really a rather modest one. He is prefacing his tendentious auto-interpretation with evidence that other authors, both sacred and profane, have had occasion to do what he claims he did in his odes. Poet and prophet alike have installed beneath their overt statements meanings inaccessible to vulgar apprehension. The notion that Dante is primarily concerned with the difference between figural and ordinary literary allegory seems to have arisen from the assumption that the phrase in his first paragraph, "the allegorical sense after the use of the poets," is simply another way of saying, "truth hidden under a beautiful fiction." That this is not very likely to have been Dante's meaning is shown by his detailed interpretation, in the fourth treatise, of Lucan's account of Marcia and Cato as an allegory on the return of the noble soul to God. One hardly thinks that Dante would have called the narrative a fiction or the method anything but the allegory of poets. This clearly suggests that the remarks about "fiction," "mantle," and Orpheus are offered by way of illustration, and that the phrase, "it is the one that" does not introduce a definition of allegory here any more than it introduces a definition of tropology in the next paragraph. Being concerned with a kind of hiding which was devised rather than discovered, Dante apparently thought it appropriate to observe that it can often be found even when the material looks most unpromisingly vain and frivolous. As an example, he cites a *bella menzogna*, an attractive pagan fable. Consequently, when Dante says that he will follow the method of the poets, he is not suggesting that the reader should, to quote Professor Singleton, "*in the act of reading*, view the literal sense [of the odes] as 'fable,' 'fiction,' 'imaginary,' and justified only if it contains a 'truth'!"[11] Does he not say that his contemporaries had, in the act of reading the odes, taken them as real love poems to a real woman; and that without the *Convivio* as a clue to his otherwise unascertainable intentions, any reader must inevitably see in them only the expression of a great and infamous passion? His gloss insists that the *donna gentile* never existed, not that she is the esthetic equivalent of the ladies of Guillaume de Lorris. Dante may really have been thinking about *Filosofia*; but that he did not put her into his poetry by means of the transparent, explicitly referential allegory of the *Roman de la Rose* and *Pilgrim's Progress* is proved by Dante's own words and the reader's own eyesight. The odes are, if you will, mannered, allusive, enigmatic, esoteric, and hyper-intellectual, but Dante clearly invites the reader to come at their ultimate meaning through a surface that is, within the limits of a very conventionalized mode of representing reality, real. And this is quite consistent with his whole conception of the allegory of poets.[12]

[11] Charles S. Singleton, "The Irreducible Dove," *Comparative Literature*, 9 (1957), 129.

[12] This appendix has appeared in a slightly different form in *Philological Quarterly*, 40 (1961), 144.

www.ingramcontent.com/pod-product-compliance
Lightning Source LLC
Chambersburg PA
CBHW021716230426
43668CB00008B/854